Right and Wrong

Basic Readings in Ethics

CHRISTINA
HOFF SOMMERS
Clark University

Under the general editorship of
ROBERT J. FOGELIN
Dartmouth College

Harcourt Brace Jovanovich, Publishers
San Diego   New York   Chicago   Austin   Washington, D.C.
London   Sydney   Tokyo   Toronto

COVER Masaccio, *The Expulsion from Eden*, fresco, c. 1425, Brancacci Chapel, Florence. Photo courtesy of Scala / Art Resource, New York.

ISBN: 0-15-577110-8

Library of Congress Catalog Card Number: 85-60810

Printed in the United States of America

Preface

This book offers a judicious selection of readings on ethical theory. Instructors of courses in medical ethics, business ethics, and contemporary moral problems typically initiate the student into the subject with a general review of ethical theory. This collection is suitable for that purpose. Alternatively, the book can serve for the ethics unit in an introductory philosophy course.

Kantianism and Utilitarianism attract a majority of academic philosophers; relativism and egoism have a large following among nonphilosophers. I have chosen to present these theories in depth rather than give sketchy treatment to a larger variety of theories. The book contains classical materials on the main positions, as well as clear and lively contemporary expositions—some of which have themselves achieved the status of classics.

My thanks to Fred Sommers for his cheerful assistance throughout, and to Stephen Tigner, University of Toledo, for his thoughtful review of the manuscript. This book is dedicated to my mother in gratitude and love.

Contents

PREFACE   iii

INTRODUCTION   1

CHAPTER 1   KANTIANISM

Good Will, Duty, and the Categorical Imperative
  Immanuel Kant   8
Kant's Ethical Theory: Exposition and Critique
  Fred Feldman   18
Respect for Persons and Fraternity
  R. S. Peters   43
What If Everyone Did That?
  Colin Strang   51
A Critique of Kantianism
  Richard Taylor   62

CHAPTER 2   UTILITARIANISM

The Principle of Utility
  Jeremy Bentham   72
Utilitarianism
  J. J. C. Smart   79
A Critique of Utilitarianism
  Bernard Williams   93
Rule-Utilitarianism
  John Hospers   102
A Defense of Utilitarianism
  R. M. Hare   121

CHAPTER 3   ETHICAL RELATIVISM

Morality as Custom
  Herodotus   132
A Defense of Ethical Relativism
  Ruth Benedict   133
Ethical Relativism: A Critique
  W. T. Stace   142
Vulgar Relativism
  Bernard Williams   155
Trying Out One's New Sword
  Mary Midgley   159

CHAPTER 4   EGOISM

Of the State of Men Without Civil Society
  Thomas Hobbes   168
The Virtue of Selfishness
  Ayn Rand   175
Egoism and Moral Skepticism
  James Rachels   179
Morality, Egoism and the Prisoner's Dilemma
  Peter Singer   192

Suggested Readings   201

INTRODUCTION

There is no way to avoid making moral judgments. Or, to be more precise, there is no way to avoid doing so without losing one's essential humanity. One sees a child being mistreated and describes the mistreatment as "cruel." That little word is value laden in two ways. First, any act of deliberate cruelty is wrong. Second, cruelty is evil, since the world would be a better place without the misery that is produced by cruel acts. The ethical thinkers we shall be studying attempt to make sense of the rights and wrongs and the goods and evils of our experience. In particular, they try to show what we mean by these terms and how we apply them in moral judgment.

When someone says, "It is wrong to be cruel to children," is that a statement of fact? Does it signify an objective state of affairs in just the way that "Everest is the tallest mountain" states an objective fact independent of what people say or think? Whether and in what sense moral judgments are objective is one of the oldest questions in moral philosophy. The reader will find here some of the answers given to this and related questions by such great moral philosophers as Immanuel Kant, Jeremy Bentham, and Thomas Hobbes, as well as by some of the leading figures in contemporary moral philosophy.

Immanuel Kant (1724–1804) located the foundations of morality in the human capacity to make rational choices. He believed that rational beings are free to act out of principle and to refrain from acting from mere impulse or the desire for pleasure. Impulse is subjective and private, but moral principles are objective and applicable to everyone. So, says Kant, in contemplating an act one must ask oneself if it is the sort of act that should be adopted by everyone. Reason prescribes respect for all persons, including oneself, as a universal principle. Persons are "ends," beings whose very existence poses limits on how they may be treated.

Kant's ethical system is attractive for its emphasis on human dignity and principled action, but many of his arguments in support of his main theses have been criticized for being obscure or fallacious. He and his followers have also been criticized for their apparent readiness to sacrifice human happiness for the sake of moral principles. Critics cite Kant's uncompromising position against lying. According to Kant, if a murderer comes to one's door and demands to know the whereabouts of an intended victim, one must not lie, no matter what the consequences. That seems obviously wrong, and Utilitarianism, a theory opposed to Kantianism, explains why.

For Kant, morality is primarily a matter of principled intention. Jeremy Bentham and John Stuart Mill, the originators of Utilitarianism, dispense with talk of duty, principles, and motives and define moral goodness in terms of happiness. In Mill's words, "Actions are right in proportion as they tend to promote happiness, wrong as they tend to produce the reverse of happiness." The rightness or wrongness of an action can be empirically determined by calculating the amount of happiness or misery that action is likely to bring about. Bentham calls this the "hedonic calculus." Cruelty, deception, and treachery are (usually) wrong, not because they cannot be willed by a rational moral agent, but because they tend to create misery. An occasional and useful deception is therefore morally permissible.

Many philosophers criticize Utilitarianism for its failure to provide an adequate account of such fundamental notions as justice and integrity. Suppose one could significantly increase human happiness by occasionally arresting and punishing innocent people. Intuitively such a practice seems wrong. Yet Utilitarianism seems to condone it. Such cases suggest that there may be more to being moral than acting to increase happiness and diminish misery. A number of contemporary moralists, among them R. M. Hare, J. J. C. Smart, and John Hospers, believe that Utilitarianism can be defended from objections of this kind.

Kantianism and Utilitarianism differ in the way they explain the propositions "X is right" and "X is wrong." But they agree that there are such things as universally applicable moral principles that transcend the beliefs and practices of particular people or groups of people. Both Kantianism and Utilitarianism would condemn a practice like human sacrifice even if it was a central norm of a whole society, as it was, say, for the Aztecs. But there is another moral theory, called Ethical Relativism, that challenges the claim that there are transcultural and objective criteria for determining right and wrong. According to the ethical relativist, each society has its own moral code, and all codes have equal claim to validity. The renowned anthropoloist Ruth Benedict maintains that what is "moral" or "good" varies from culture to culture. Thus Benedict says, "Mankind has always preferred to say, 'It is morally good,' rather than 'It is habitual.' . . . But historically the two phrases are synonymous."

Ethical Relativism does appeal to our desire to be respectful and tolerant of other cultures. But, as Mary Midgley and Bernard Williams point out, the price of tolerating all exotic practices is callousness. In tolerating the norms of all social systems, one morally acquiesces to the misery of the slave and the terror and death of the sacrificial victim. One reads the following in the United Nations Declaration on the Rights of Children:

> The child shall be given the opportunity . . . to develop physically, morally, spiritually and socially in a healthy and normal manner and in conditions of freedom and dignity.

Kantianism and Utilitarianism, in their different ways, provide grounds for condemning any society that falls short of this ideal. But many philosophers maintain that Ethical Relativism cannot consistently condemn the mistreatment of children where such mistreatment is a norm of a particular culture.

Another doctrine we consider is known as egoism. *Psychological* egoism maintains that human beings always act from a single motive: self-love. This belief is not so much a philosophical theory as an empirical generalization about human behavior that has influenced the way some philosophers approach the concept of right and wrong. The great seventeenth-century philosopher Thomas Hobbes is associated with this view. According to Hobbes, morality is grounded in a "social contract" that persons enter into "not so much for love of our fellows, as for the love of ourselves." Most contemporary philosophers dismiss egoism as an oversimple theory of human behavior. Self-love is only one of several reasons for acting; others include compassion, malice, and self-hatred. Psychological egoism has also been criticized by some modern biologists, who argue that altruism has significant survival value.

Ethical egoism is more directly a moral theory. According to the ethical egoist, all obligations reduce to one: act in such a way as to promote your own best interests. Ethical egoists tell us how human beings *should* act; these philosophers are not committed to the empirical proposition that humans always *do* act out of self-interest. Contemporary proponents of egoism, such as Ayn Rand and Harry Browne, see altruistic theories like Kantianism and Utilitarianism as positing unrealistic ideals that weaken people and engender guilt and cynicism. James Rachels, who rejects all forms of egoism, believes that ethical egoism cannot be formally refuted. But he argues that, consistently practiced, the doctrine has unacceptable consequences.

A final introductory word. Since we constantly pass moral judgment on ourselves and others, it is clearly desirable to do so fairly and intelligently. This book presents the work of some of the most influential moral philosophers of the past and present. Reading what they have to say is an obvious first step to practical wisdom.

Chapter

1

KANTIANISM

Good Will, Duty, and the Categorical Imperative

IMMANUEL KANT

Immanuel Kant (1724–1804) is considered to be one of the greatest philosophers of all time. He lived in Königsberg, in East Prussia and was a professor at the university there. Kant made significant and highly original contributions to esthetics, jurisprudence, and the philosophy of religion, as well as to ethics and epistemology. His best-known works are the *Critique of Pure Reason* and the *Foundations of the Metaphysics of Morals.*

Human beings have desires and appetites. They are also rational, capable of knowing what is right and capable of willing to do it. They can therefore exercise their wills in the rational control of desire for the purpose of right action. This is what persons of moral worth do. According to Kant, to possess moral worth is more important than to possess intelligence, humor, strength, or any other talent of the mind or body. These talents are valuable, but moral worth has *absolute* value, commanding not mere admiration but reverence and respect. Human beings who do right merely because it pleases them are not yet intrinsically moral. For had it pleased them they would have done wrong. To act morally is to act from no other motive than the motive of doing what is right. This kind of motive has nothing to do with anything as

GOOD WILL, DUTY, AND THE CATEGORICAL IMPERATIVE   From *Fundamental Principles of the Metaphysics of Morals* by Immanuel Kant, sections 1 and 2. Translated by T. K. Abbott (1898). Original footnotes have been omitted.

subjective as pleasure. To do right out of principle is to recognize an objective right that poses an obligation on any rational being. Moral persons act in such a way that they could will that the principles of their actions should be universal laws for everyone else as well. This is one test of a moral act: Is it the kind of act that everyone should perform? Kant illustrates how this test can be applied to determine whether a given principle is moral and objective or merely subjective. For example, I may wish to break a promise, but that cannot be moral since I cannot will that promise-breaking be a universal practice.

Universal principles impose *categorical* imperatives. An imperative is a demand that I act in a certain fashion. For example, if I want to buy a house, it is imperative that I learn something about houses. But "Learn about houses" is a *hypothetical* imperative since it is *conditional* on my wanting to buy a house. A *categorical* imperative is unconditional. An example is "Keep your promises." Thus an imperative is not preceded by any condition, such as "if you want a good reputation." Hypothetical imperatives are "prudential": "If you want security, buy theft insurance." Categorical imperatives are moral: "Do not lie." Kant argues that the categorical imperative presupposes the absolute worth of all rational beings as ends in themselves. Thus another formulation of the categorical imperative is "So act as to treat humanity . . . as an end withal, never as a means only." Kant calls the domain of beings that are to be treated in this way the "kingdom of ends."

Nothing can possibly be conceived in the world, or even out of it, which can be called good, without qualification, except a Good Will. Intelligence, wit, judgment, and the other *talents* of the mind, however they may be named, or courage, resolution, perseverance, as qualities of temperament, are undoubtedly good and desirable in many respects; but these gifts of nature may also become extremely bad and mischievous if the will which is to make use of them, and

9

which, therefore, constitutes what is called *character*, is not good. It is the same with the *gifts of fortune*. Power, riches, honour, even health, and the general well-being and contentment with one's condition which is called *happiness*, inspire pride, and often presumption, if there is not a good will to correct the influence of these on the mind, and with this also to rectify the whole principle of acting, and adapt it to its end. The sight of a being who is not adorned with a single feature of a pure and good will, enjoying unbroken prosperity, can never give pleasure to an impartial rational spectator. Thus a good will appears to constitute the indispensable condition even of being worthy of happiness.

There are even some qualities which are of service to this good will itself, and may facilitate its action, yet which have no intrinsic unconditional value, but always presuppose a good will, and this qualifies the esteem that we justly have for them, and does not permit us to regard them as absolutely good. Moderation in the affections and passions, self-control, and calm deliberation are not only good in many respects, but even seem to constitute part of the intrinsic worth of the person; but they are far from deserving to be called good without qualification, although they have been so unconditionally praised by the ancients. For without the principles of a good will, they may become extremely bad; and the coolness of a villain not only makes him far more dangerous, but also directly makes him more abominable in our eyes than he would have been without it.

A good will is good not because of what it performs or effects, not by its aptness for the attainment of some proposed end, but simply by virtue of the volition, that is, it is good in itself, and considered by itself is to be esteemed much higher than all that can be brought about by it in favour of any inclination, nay, even of the sum-total of all inclinations. Even if it should happen that, owing to special disfavour of fortune, or the niggardly provision of a step-motherly nature, this will should wholly lack power to accomplish its purpose, if with its greatest efforts it should yet achieve nothing, and there should remain only the good will (not, to be sure, a mere wish, but the summoning of all means in our power), then, like a jewel, it would still shine by its own light, as a thing which has its whole value in itself. Its usefulness or fruitlessness can neither add to nor take away anything from this value.

Thus the moral worth of an action does not lie in the effect expected from it, nor in any principle of action which requires to borrow its motive from this expected effect. For all these effects— agreeableness of one's condition, and even the promotion of the happiness of others—could have been also brought about by other causes, so that for this there would have been no need of the will of a rational being; whereas it is in this alone that the supreme and unconditional good can be found. The pre-eminent good which we call moral can therefore consist in nothing else than *the conception of law* in itself, *which certainly is only possible in a rational being*, in so far as this conception, and not the expected effect, determines the will. This is a good which is already present in the person who acts accordingly, and we have not to wait for it to appear first in the result.

But what sort of law can that be, the conception of which must determine the will, even without paying any regard to the effect expected from it, in order that this will may be called good absolutely and without qualification? As I have deprived the will of every impulse which could arise to it from obedience to any law, there remains nothing but the universal conformity of its actions to law in general, which alone is to serve the will as a principle, *i.e.* I am never to act otherwise than *so that I could also will that my maxim should become a universal law.* Here, now, it is the simple conformity to law in general, without assuming any particular law applicable to certain actions, that serves the will as its principle, and must so serve it, if duty is not to be a vain delusion and a chimerical notion. The common reason of men in its practical judgments perfectly coincides with this and always has in view the principle here suggested. Let the question be, for example: May I when in distress make a promise with the intention not to keep it? I readily distinguish here between the two significations which the question may have: Whether it is prudent, or whether it is right, to make a false promise? The former may undoubtedly often be the case. I see clearly indeed that it is not enough to extricate myself from a present difficulty by means of this subterfuge, but it must be well considered whether there may not hereafter spring from this lie much greater inconvenience than that from which I now free myself, and as, with all my supposed *cunning*, the consequences cannot be so easily foreseen but that credit once lost may be much more injurious to me than any mischief which I seek to avoid at present, it should be considered whether it would not be more *prudent* to act herein according to a universal maxim, and to make it a habit to promise nothing except with the intention of keeping it. But it is soon clear to me that such a maxim will still only be based on the fear of consequences. Now it is a wholly different thing to be truthful from duty, and to be so from apprehension of injurious consequences. In the first case, the very notion of the action already implies a law for me; in the second case, I must first look about elsewhere to see what results may be combined with it which would affect myself. For to deviate from the principle of duty is beyond all doubt wicked; but to be unfaithful to my maxim of prudence may often be very advantageous to me, although to abide by it is certainly safer. The shortest way, however, and an unerring one, to discover the answer to this question whether a lying promise is consistent with duty, is to ask myself, Should I be content that my maxim (to extricate myself from difficulty by a false promise) should hold good as a universal law, for myself as well as for others? and should I be able to say to myself, "Every one may make a deceitful promise when he finds himself in a difficulty from which he cannot otherwise extricate himself?" Then I presently become aware that while I can will the lie, I can by no means will that lying should be a universal law. For with such a law there would be no promises at all, since it would be in vain to allege my intention in regard to my future actions to those who would not believe this allegation, or if they over-hastily did so, would pay me back in my own coin. Hence my maxim, as soon as it should be made a universal law, would necessarily destroy itself.

I do not, therefore, need any far-reaching penetration to discern what I have to do in order that my will may be morally good. Inexperienced in the course of the world, incapable of being prepared for all its contingencies, I only ask myself: Canst thou also will that thy maxim should be a universal law? If not, then it must be rejected, and that not because of a disadvantage accruing from it to myself or even to others, but because it cannot enter as a principle into a possible universal legislation, and reason extorts from me immediate respect for such legislation. I do not indeed as yet *discern* on what this respect is based (this the philosopher may inquire), but at least I understand this, that it is an estimation of the worth which far outweighs all worth of what is recommended by inclination, and that the necessity of acting from *pure* respect for the practical law is what constitutes duty, to which every other motive must give place, because it is the condition of a will being good *in itself*, and the worth of such a will is above everything. . . .

. . . Everything in nature works according to laws. Rational beings alone have the faculty of acting according *to the conception* of laws, that is according to principles, *i.e.* have a *will*. Since the deduction of actions from principles requires *reason*, the will is nothing but practical reason. If reason infallibly determines the will, then the actions of such a being which are recognized as objectively necessary are subjectively necessary also, *i.e.* the will is a faculty to choose *that only* which reason independent on inclination recognizes as practically necessary, *i.e.* as good. But if reason of itself does not sufficiently determine the will, if the latter is subject also to subjective conditions (particular impulses) which do not always coincide with the objective conditions; in a word, if the will does not *in itself* completely accord with reason (which is actually the case with men), then the actions which objectively are recognized as necessary are subjectively contingent, and the determination of such a will according to objective laws is *obligation*, that is to say, the relation of the objective laws to a will that is not thoroughly good is conceived as the determination of the will of a rational being by principles of reason, but which the will from its nature does not of necessity follow.

The conception of an objective principle, in so far as it is obligatory for a will, is called a command (of reason), and the formula of the command is called an Imperative. . . .

Now all *imperatives* command either *hypothetically* or *categorically*. The former represent the practical necessity of a possible action as means to something else that is willed (or at least which one might possibly will). The categorical imperative would be that which represented an action as necessary of itself without reference to another end, *i.e.*, as objectively necessary.

Since every practical law represents a possible action as good, and on this account, for a subject who is practically determinable by reason, necessary, all imperatives are formulae determining an action which is necessary according to the principle of a will good in some respects. If now the action is good only as a means *to something else*, then the imperative is *hypothetical*; if it is conceived as good *in itself* and consequently as being necessarily the principle of a will which of itself conforms to reason, then it is *categorical*. . . .

When I conceive a hypothetical imperative, in general I do not know beforehand what it will contain until I am given the condition. But when I conceive a categorical imperative, I know at once what it contains. For as the imperative contains besides the law only the necessity that the maxims shall conform to this law, while the law contains no conditions restricting it, there remains nothing but the general statement that the maxim of the action should conform to a universal law, and it is this conformity alone that the imperative properly represents as necessary.

. . . There is but one categorical imperative, namely, this: *Act only on that maxim whereby thou canst at the same time will that it should become a universal law.*

Now if all imperatives of duty can be deduced from this one imperative as from their principle, then, although it should remain undecided whether what is called duty is not merely a vain notion, yet at least we shall be able to show what we understand by it and what this notion means.

Since the universality of the law according to which effects are produced constitutes what is properly called *nature* in the most general sense (as to form), that is the existence of things so far as it is determined by general laws, the imperative of duty may be expressed thus: *Act as if the maxim of thy action were to become by thy will a universal law of nature.*

We will now enumerate a few duties, adopting the usual division of them into duties to ourselves and to others, and into perfect and imperfect duties.

1. A man reduced to despair by a series of misfortunes feels wearied of life, but is still so far in possession of his reason that he can ask himself whether it would not be contrary to his duty to himself to take his own life. Now he inquires whether the maxim of his action could become a universal law of nature. His maxim is: From self-love I adopt it as a principle to shorten my life when its longer duration is likely to bring more evil than satisfaction. It is asked then simply whether this principle founded on self-love can become a universal law of nature. Now we see at once that a system of nature of which it should be a law to destroy life by means of the

very feeling whose special nature it is to impel to the improvement of life would contradict itself, and therefore could not exist as a system of nature; hence that maxim cannot possibly exist as a universal law of nature, and consequently would be wholly inconsistent with the supreme principle of all duty.

2. Another finds himself forced by necessity to borrow money. He knows that he will not be able to repay it, but sees also that nothing will be lent to him, unless he promises stoutly to repay it in a definite time. He desires to make this promise, but he has still so much conscience as to ask himself: Is it not unlawful and inconsistent with duty to get out of a difficulty in this way? Suppose, however, that he resolves to do so, then the maxim of his action would be expressed thus: When I think myself in want of money, I will borrow money and promise to repay it, although I know that I never can do so. Now this principle of self-love or of one's own advantage may perhaps be consistent with my whole future welfare; but the question now is, Is it right? I change then the suggestion of self-love into a universal law, and state the question thus: How would it be if my maxim were a universal law? Then I see at once that it could never hold as a universal law of nature, but would necessarily contradict itself. For supposing it to be a universal law that everyone when he thinks himself in a difficulty should be able to promise whatever he pleases, with the purpose of not keeping his promise, the promise itself would become impossible, as well as the end that one might have in view in it, since no one would consider that anything was promised to him, but would ridicule all such statements as vain pretences.

3. A third finds in himself a talent which with the help of some culture might make him a useful man in many respects. But he finds himself in comfortable circumstances, and prefers to indulge in pleasure rather than to take pains in enlarging and improving his happy natural capacities. He asks, however, whether this maxim of neglect of his natural gifts, besides agreeing with his inclination to indulgence, agrees also with what is called duty. He sees then that a system of nature could indeed subsist with such a universal law although men (like the South Sea islanders) should let their talents rest, and resolve to devote their lives merely to idleness, amusement, and propagation of their species—in a word, to enjoyment; but he cannot possibly *will* that this should be a universal law of

nature, or be implanted in us as such by a natural instinct. For, as a rational being, he necessarily wills that his faculties be developed, since they serve him, and have been given him, for all sorts of possible purposes.

4. A fourth, who is in prosperity, while he sees that others have to contend with great wretchedness and that he could help them, thinks: What concern is it of mine? Let everyone be as happy as Heaven pleases, or as he can make himself; I will take nothing from him nor even envy him, only I do not wish to contribute anything to his welfare or to his assistance in distress! Now no doubt if such a mode of thinking were a universal law, the human race might very well subsist, and doubtless even better than in a state in which everyone talks of sympathy and good-will, or even takes care occasionally to put it into practice, but, on the other side, also cheats when he can, betrays the rights of men, or otherwise violates them. But although it is possible that a universal law of nature might exist in accordance with that maxim, it is impossible to *will* that such a principle should have the universal validity of a law of nature. For a will which resolved this would contradict itself, inasmuch as many cases might occur in which one would have need of the love and sympathy of others, and in which, by such a law of nature, sprung from his own will, he would deprive himself of all hope of the aid he desires. . . .

We have thus established at least this much, that if duty is a conception which is to have any import and real legislative authority for our actions, it can only be expressed in categorical, and not at all in hypothetical imperatives. We have also, which is of great importance, exhibited clearly and definitely for every practical application the content of the categorical imperative, which must contain the principle of all duty if there is such a thing at all. We have not yet, however, advanced so far as to prove *à priori* that there actually is such an imperative, that there is a practical law which commands absolutely of itself, and without any other impulse, and that the following of this law is duty. . . .

Now I say: man and generally any rational being *exists* as an end in himself, *not merely as a means* to be arbitrarily used by this or that will, but in all his actions, whether they concern himself or other rational beings, must be always regarded at the same time as an end. All objects of the inclinations have only a conditional worth;

for if the inclinations and the wants founded on them did not exist, then their object would be without value. But the inclinations themselves being sources of want are so far from having an absolute worth for which they should be desired, that, on the contrary, it must be the universal wish of every rational being to be wholly free from them. Thus the worth of any object which is *to be acquired* by our action is always conditional. Beings whose existence depends not on our will but on nature's, have nevertheless, if they are rational beings, only a relative value as means, and are therefore called *things*; rational beings, on the contrary, are called *persons*, because their very nature points them out as ends in themselves, that is as something which must not be used merely as means, and so far therefore restricts freedom of action (and is an object of respect). These, therefore, are not merely subjective ends whose existence has a worth *for us* as an effect of our action, but *objective ends*, that is things whose existence is an end in itself: an end moreover for which no other can be substituted, which they should subserve *merely* as means, for otherwise nothing whatever would possess *absolute worth*; but if all worth were conditioned and therefore contingent, then there would be no supreme practical principle of reason whatever.

If then there is a supreme practical principle or, in respect of the human will, a categorical imperative, it must be one which, being drawn from the conception of that which is necessarily an end for everyone because it is *an end in itself,* constitutes an *objective* principle of will, and can therefore serve as a universal practical law. The foundation of this principle is: *rational nature exists as an end in itself.* Man necessarily conceives his own existence as being so: so far then this is a *subjective* principle of human actions. But every other rational being regards its existence similarly, just on the same rational principle that holds for me: so that it is at the same time an objective principle, from which as a supreme practical law all laws of the will must be capable of being deduced. Accordingly the practical imperative will be as follows: *So act as to treat humanity, whether in thine own person or in that of any other, in every case as an end withal, never as means only. . . .*

The conception of every rational being as one which must consider itself as giving in all the maxims of its will universal laws, so as to judge itself and its actions from this point of view—this

conception leads to another which depends on it and is very fruit-
ful, namely, that of a *kingdom of ends*.

By a *kingdom* I understand the union of different rational beings
in a system by common laws. Now since it is by laws that ends are
determined as regards their universal validity, hence, if we abstract
from the personal differences of rational beings, and likewise from
all the content of their private ends, we shall be able to conceive all
ends combined in a systematic whole (including both rational
beings as ends in themselves, and also the special ends which each
may propose to himself), that is to say, we can conceive a kingdom
of ends, which on the preceding principles is possible.

For all rational beings come under the *law* that each of them must
treat itself and all others *never merely as means*, but in every case *at
the same time as ends in themselves*. Hence results a systematic union
of rational beings by common objective laws, *i.e.*, a kingdom
which may be called a kingdom of ends. . . .

Kant's Ethical Theory: Exposition and Critique

FRED FELDMAN

Fred Feldman (b. 1941) is a professor of philosophy at the
University of Massachusetts, Amherst. His books include *Introductory Ethics, A Cartesian Introduction to Philosophy*, and *Doing the Best We Can*.

Feldman's exposition of Kant's moral theory begins
with a popular and rough version of what Kant calls the
supreme principle of morality: "If you wouldn't want
everyone else to act in a certain way, then you shouldn't
act in that way yourself." Feldman goes on to discuss
several more-refined formulations of this general idea.

KANT'S ETHICAL THEORY From *Introduction to Ethics* by Fred Feldman, © 1978, pp. 97, 98, 99,
101–14, 119–23, 133, 134. Reprinted by permission of Prentice-Hall, Inc., Englewood Cliffs, N.J.

For Kant, any maxim (rule) that we use to guide our actions morally must be "universalizable": it must be a maxim that we can "will" to be universally adopted by all moral agents. Kant calls this requirement the categorical imperative. Feldman examines the four cases that Kant presents in his attempt to show how the categorical imperative works in real-life situations. Feldman finds that Kant's general position is profound and of central importance, but that all too often the arguments, and even his position, are confused, obscure, and logically flawed.

Sometimes our moral thinking takes a decidedly nonutilitarian turn. That is, we often seem to appeal to a principle that is inconsistent with the whole utilitarian standpoint. One case in which this occurs clearly enough is the familiar tax-cheat case. A person decides to cheat on his income tax, rationalizing his misbehavior as follows: "The government will not be injured by the absence of my tax money. After all, compared with the enormous total they take in, my share is really a negligible sum. On the other hand, I will be happier if I have the use of the money. Hence, no one will be injured by my cheating, and one person will be better off. Thus, it is better for me to cheat than it is for me to pay."

In response to this sort of reasoning, we may be inclined to say something like this: "Perhaps you are right in thinking that you will be better off if you cheat. And perhaps you are right in thinking that the government won't even know the difference. Nevertheless, your act would be wrong. For if everyone were to cheat on his income taxes, the government would soon go broke. Surely you can see that you wouldn't want others to act in the way you propose to act. So you shouldn't act in that way." While it may not be clear that this sort of response would be decisive, it should be clear that this is an example of a sort of response that is often given.

There are several things to notice about this response. For one, it is not based on the view that the example of the tax cheat will provoke everyone else to cheat too. If that were the point of the response, then the response might be explained on the basis of utilitarian considerations. We could understand the responder to be saying that the tax cheater has miscalculated his utilities. Whereas he thinks his act of cheating has high utility, in fact it has low utility because it will eventually result in the collapse of the government. It is important to recognize that the response presented above is not based upon any such utilitarian considerations. This can be seen by reflecting on the fact that the point could just as easily have been made in this way: "Of course, very few other people will know about your cheating, and so your behavior will not constitute an example to others. Thus, it will not provoke others to cheat. Nevertheless, your act is wrong. For if everyone were to cheat as you propose to do, then the government would collapse. Since you wouldn't want others to behave in the way you propose to behave, you should not behave in that way. It would be wrong to cheat."

Another thing to notice about the response in this case is that the responder has not simply said, "What you propose to do would be cheating; hence, it is wrong." The principle in question is not simply the principle that cheating is wrong. Rather, the responder has appealed to a much more general principle, which seems to be something like this: If you wouldn't want everyone else to act in a certain way, then you shouldn't act in that way yourself.

This sort of general principle is in fact used quite widely in our moral reasoning. If someone proposes to remove the pollution-control devices from his automobile, his friends are sure to say "What if everyone did that?" They would have in mind some dire consequences for the quality of the air, but their point would not be that the removal of the pollution-control device by one person will in fact cause others to remove theirs, and will thus eventually lead to the destruction of the environment. Their point, rather, is that if their friend would not want others to act in the way he proposes to act, then it would be wrong for him to act in that way. This principle is also used against the person who refrains from giving to charity; the person who evades the draft in time of national emergency; the person who tells a lie in order to get out of a bad spot; and even the person who walks across a patch of newly seeded grass. In all such cases, we feel that the person acts wrongly not because his actions will have bad results, but because he wouldn't want others to behave in the way he behaves.

A highly refined version of this nonutilitarian principle is the heart of the moral theory of Immanuel Kant.[1] In his *Groundwork of the Metaphysic of Morals*,[2] Kant presents, develops, and defends the thesis that something like this principle is the "supreme principle of morality." Kant's presentation is rather complex; in parts, it is very hard to follow. Part of the trouble arises from his use of a rather unfamiliar technical vocabulary. Another source of trouble is that Kant is concerned with establishing a variety of other points in this little book, and some of these involve fairly complex issues in metaphysics and epistemology. Since our aim here is simply to present a clear, concise account of Kant's basic moral doctrine, we will have to ignore quite a bit of what he says in the book.

Kant formulates his main principle in a variety of different ways. All of the members of the following set of formulations seem to have a lot in common:

> I ought never to act except in such a way that I can also will that my maxim should become a universal law.[3]
>
> Act only on that maxim through which you can at the same time will that it should become a universal law.[4]
>
> Act as if the maxim of your action were to become through your will a universal law of nature.[5]
>
> We must be able to will that a maxim of our action should become a universal law—this is the general canon for all moral judgment of action.[6]

Before we can evaluate this principle, which Kant calls the *categorical imperative*, we have to devote some attention to figuring out what it is supposed to mean. To do this, we must answer a variety of questions. What is a maxim? What is meant by "universal law"? What does Kant mean by "will"? Let us consider these questions in turn.

---

[1]Immanuel Kant (1724–1804) is one of the greatest Continental philosophers. He produced quite a few philosophical works of major importance. The *Critique of Pure Reason* (1781) is perhaps his most famous work.

[2]Kant's *Grundlegung zur Metaphysik der Sitten* (1785) has been translated into English many times. All references here are to Immanuel Kant, *Groundwork of the Metaphysic of Morals*, translated and analysed by H. J. Paton (New York: Harper & Row, 1964).

[3]Kant, *Groundwork*, p. 70.

[4]*Ibid.*, p. 88.

[5]*Ibid.*, p. 89.

[6]*Ibid.*, p. 91.

Maxims

In a footnote, Kant defines *maxim* as "a subjective principle of volition."[7] This definition is hardly helpful. Perhaps we can do better. First, however, a little background.

Kant apparently believes that when a person engages in genuine action, he always acts on some sort of general principle. The general principle will explain what the person takes himself to be doing and the circumstances in which he takes himself to be doing it. For example, if I need money, and can get some only by borrowing it, even though I know I won't be able to repay it, I might proceed to borrow some from a friend. My maxim in performing this act might be, "Whenever I need money and can get it by borrowing it, then I will borrow it, even if I know I won't be able to repay it."

Notice that this maxim is *general*. If I adopt it, I commit myself to behaving in the described way *whenever* I need money and the other conditions are satisfied. In this respect, the maxim serves to formulate a general principle of action rather than just some narrow reason applicable in just one case.[8] So a maxim must describe some general sort of situation, and then propose some form of action for the situation. To adopt a maxim is to commit yourself to acting in the described way whenever the situation in question arises. . . .

For our purposes, it will be useful to introduce a concept that Kant does not employ. This is the concept of the *generalized form* of a maxim. Suppose I decide to go to sleep one night and my maxim in performing this act is this:

M_3:   Whenever I am tired, I shall sleep.

My maxim is stated in such a way as to contain explicit references to me. It contains two occurrences of the word "I." The generalized form of my maxim is the principle we would get if we were to revise my maxim so as to make it applicable to everyone. Thus, the generalized form of my maxim is this:

GM_3:   Whenever anyone is tired, he will sleep.

---

[7]*Ibid.*, p. 69n.

[8]In some unusual cases, it may accidentally happen that the situation to which the maxim applies can occur only once, as, for example, in the case of successful suicide. Nevertheless, the maxim is general in form.

In general, then we can represent the form of a maxim in this way:

> *M:* Whenever I am ———, I shall ———.

Actual maxims have descriptions of situations in the first blank and descriptions of actions in the second blank. The generalized form of a maxim can be represented in this way:

> *GM:* Whenever anyone is ———, she will ———.

So much, then, for maxims. Let us turn to our second question, "What is meant by universal law?"

Universal Law

When, in the formulation of the categorical imperative, Kant speaks of "universal law," he seems to have one or the other of two things in mind. Sometimes he seems to be thinking of a *universal law of nature*, and sometimes he seems to be thinking of a *universal law of freedom*.

A *law of nature* is a fully general statement that describes not only how things are, but how things always *must* be. Consider this example: If the temperature of a gas in an enclosed container is increased, then the pressure will increase too. This statement accurately describes the behavior of gases in enclosed containers. Beyond this, however, it describes behavior that is, in a certain sense, necessary. The pressure not only *does* increase, but it *must* increase if the volume remains the same and the temperature is increased. This "must" expresses not logical or moral necessity, but "physical necessity." Thus, a law of nature is a fully general statement that expresses a physical necessity.

A *universal law of freedom* is a universal principle describing how all people ought to act in a certain circumstance. It does not have to be a legal enactment—it needn't be passed by Congress or signed by the president. Furthermore, some universal laws of freedom are not always followed—although they should be. If in fact it is true that all promises ought to be kept, then this principle is a universal law of freedom: If anyone has made a promise, he keeps it. The "must" in a statement such as "If you have made a promise, then you must keep it" does not express logical or physical necessity. It may be said to express moral necessity. Using this concept of moral necessity, we can say that a universal law of freedom is a fully general statement that expresses a moral necessity.

Sometimes Kant's categorical imperative is stated in terms of universal laws of nature, and sometimes in terms of universal laws of freedom. We will consider the "law of nature" version, since Kant appeals to it in discussing some fairly important examples.

Willing

To will that something be the case is more than to merely wish for it to be the case. A person might wish that there would be peace everywhere in the world. Yet knowing that it is not within his power to bring about this wished-for state of affairs, he might refrain from willing that there be peace everywhere in the world. It is not easy to say just what a person does when he wills that something be the case. According to one view, willing that something be the case is something like commanding yourself to make it be the case. So if I will my arm to go up, that would be something like commanding myself to raise my arm. The Kantian concept of willing is a bit more complicated, however. According to Kant, it makes sense to speak of willing something to happen, even if that something is not an action. For example, we can speak of someone willing that everyone keep their promises.

Some states of affairs are impossible. They simply cannot occur. For example, consider the state of affairs of your jumping up and down while remaining perfectly motionless. It simply cannot be done. Yet a sufficiently foolish or irrational person might will that such a state of affairs occur. That would be as absurd as commanding someone else to jump up and down while remaining motionless. Kant would say of a person who has willed in this way that his will has "contradicted itself." We can also put the point by saying that the person has willed inconsistently.

Inconsistency in willing can arise in another, somewhat less obvious way. Suppose a person has already willed that he remain motionless. He does not change this volition, but persists in willing that he remain motionless. At the same time, however, he begins to will that he jump up and down. Although each volition is self-consistent, it is inconsistent to will both of them at the same time. This is a second way in which inconsistency in willing can arise.

It may be the case that there are certain things that everyone must always will. For example, we may have to will that we avoid intense pain. Anyone who wills something that is inconsistent with something everyone must will, thereby wills inconsistently.

Some of Kant's examples suggest that he held that inconsistency in willing can arise in a third way. This form of inconsistency is a bit more complex to describe. Suppose a person wills to be in Boston on Monday and also wills to be in San Francisco on Tuesday. Suppose, furthermore, that because of certain foul-ups at the airport it will be impossible for her to get from Boston to San Francisco on Tuesday. In this case, Kant would perhaps say that the person has willed inconsistently.

In general, we can say that a person wills inconsistently if he wills that p be the case and he wills that q be the case and it is impossible for p and q to be the case together.

The Categorical Imperative

With all this background, we may be in a position to interpret the first version of Kant's categorical imperative. Our interpretation is this:

> CI_1: An act is morally right if and only if the agent of the act can consistently will that the generalized form of the maxim of the act be a law of nature.

We can simplify our formulation slightly by introducing a widely used technical term. We can say that a maxim is *universalizable* if and only if the agent who acts upon it can consistently will that its generalized form be a law of nature. Making use of this new term, we can restate our first version of the categorical imperative as follows:

> CI_1': An act is morally right if and only if its maxim is universalizable.

As formulated here, the categorical imperative is a statement of necessary and sufficient conditions for the moral rightness of actions. Some commentators have claimed that Kant did not intend his principle to be understood in this way. They have suggested that Kant meant it to be understood merely as a necessary but not sufficient condition for morally right action. Thus, they would prefer to formulate the imperative in some way such as this:

CI_1'': An act is morally right only if its maxim is universalizable.

Understood in this way, the categorical imperative points out one thing to avoid in action. That is, it tells us to avoid actions whose maxims cannot be universalized. But it does not tell us the distinguishing feature of the actions we should perform. Thus, it does not provide us with a criterion of morally right action. Since Kant explicitly affirms that his principle is "the supreme principle of morality," it is reasonable to suppose that he intended it to be taken as a statement of necessary and sufficient conditions for morally right action. In any case, we will take the first version of the categorical imperative to be CI_1 rather than CI_1''.

It is interesting to note that other commentators have claimed that the categorical imperative isn't a criterion of right action at all. They have claimed that it was intended to be understood as a criterion of correctness for *maxims*.[9] These commentators might formulate the principle in this way:

CI_1''': A maxim is morally acceptable if and only if it is universalizable.

This interpretation is open to a variety of objections. In the first place, it is not supported by the text. Kant repeatedly states that the categorical imperative is the basic principle by which we are to evaluate actions.[10] Furthermore, when he presents his formulations of the categorical imperative, he generally states it as a principle about the moral rightness of action. Finally, it is somewhat hard to see why we should be interested in the principle such as CI_1'''. For it does not constitute a theory about right action, or good persons, or anything else that has traditionally been a subject of moral enquiry. CI_1, on the other hand, competes directly with act utilitarianism, rule utilitarianism, and other classical moral theories. . . .

---

[9]See, for example, Robert Paul Wolff, *The Autonomy of Reason* (New York: Harper & Row, 1973), p. 163.
[10]This is stated especially clearly on p. 107 of the *Groundwork*.

Kant's Four Examples

In a very famous passage in Chapter 11 of the *Groundwork*, Kant presents four illustrations of the application of the categorical imperative.[11] In each case, in Kant's opinion, the act is morally wrong and the maxim is not universalizable. Thus, Kant holds that his theory implies that each of these acts is wrong. If Kant is right about this, then he has given us four positive instances of his theory. That is, he has given us four cases in which his theory yields correct results. Unfortunately, the illustrations are not entirely persuasive.

Kant distinguishes between "duties to self" and "duties to others." He also distinguishes between "perfect" and "imperfect" duties. This gives him four categories of duty: "perfect to self," "perfect to others," "imperfect to self," and "imperfect to others." Kant gives one example of each type of duty. By "perfect duty," Kant says he means a duty "which admits of no exception in the interests of inclination."[12] Kant seems to have in mind something like this: If a person has a perfect duty to perform a certain kind of action, then he must *always* do that kind of action when the opportunity arises. For example, Kant apparently holds that we must always perform the (negative) action of refraining from committing suicide. This would be a perfect duty. On the other hand, if a person has an imperfect duty to do a kind of action, then he must at least *sometimes* perform an action of that kind when the opportunity arises. For example, Kant maintains that we have an imperfect duty to help others in distress. We should devote at least some of our time to charitable activities, but we are under no obligation to give all of our time to such work.

The perfect/imperfect distinction has been drawn in a variety of ways—none of them entirely clear. Some commentators have said that if a person has a perfect duty to do a certain action, *a*, then there must be someone else who has a corresponding right to demand that *a* be done. This seems to be the case in Kant's second example, but not in the first example. Thus, it isn't clear that we should understand the concept of perfect duty in this way.

---

[11]Kant, *Groundwork*, pp. 89–91.
[12]*Ibid.*, p. 89n.

Although the perfect/imperfect distinction is fairly interesting in itself, it does not play a major role in Kant's theory. Kant introduces the distinction primarily to insure that his examples will illustrate different kinds of duty.

Kant's first example illustrates the application of CI_1 to a case of perfect duty to oneself—the alleged duty to refrain from committing suicide. Kant describes the miserable state of the person contemplating suicide, and tries to show that his categorical imperative entails that the person should not take his own life. In order to simplify our discussion, let us use the abbreviation "a_1" to refer to the act of suicide the man would commit, if he were to commit suicide. According to Kant, every act must have a maxim. Kant tells us the maxim of a_1: "From self-love I make it my principle to shorten my life if its continuance threatens more evil than it promises pleasure."[13] Let us simplify and clarify this maxim, understanding it as follows:

$M(a_1)$: When continuing to live will bring me more pain than pleasure, I shall commit suicide out of self-love.

The generalized form of this maxim is as follows:

$GM(a_1)$: Whenever continuing to live will bring anyone more pain than pleasure, he will commit suicide out of self-love.

Since Kant believes that suicide is wrong, he attempts to show that his moral principle, the categorical imperative, entails that a_1 is wrong. To do this, of course, he needs to show that the agent of a_1 cannot consistently will that $GM(a_1)$ be a law of nature. Kant tries to show this in the following passage:

. . . a system of nature by whose law the very same feeling whose function is to stimulate the furtherance of life should actually destroy life would contradict itself and consequently could not subsist as a system of nature. Hence this maxim cannot possibly hold as a universal law of nature and is therefore entirely opposed to the supreme principle of all duty.[14]

The general outline of Kant's argument is clear enough:

---
[13]*Ibid.*, p. 89.
[14]*Ibid.*

Suicide Example

(1) $GM(a_1)$ cannot be a law of nature.
(2) If $GM(a_1)$ cannot be a law of nature, then the agent of a_1 cannot consistently will that $GM(a_1)$ be a law of nature.
(3) a_1 is morally right if and only if the agent of a_1 can consistently will that $GM(a_1)$ be a law of nature.
(4) Therefore, a_1 is not morally right.

In order to determine whether Kant really has shown that his theory entails that a_1 is not right, let us look at this argument more closely. First of all, for our purposes we can agree that the argument is valid. If all the premises are true, then the argument shows that the imagined act of suicide would not be right. CI_1, here being used as premise (3), would thus be shown to imply that a_1 is not right.

Since we are now interested primarily in seeing how Kant makes use of CI_1, we can withhold judgment on the merits of it for the time being.

The second premise seems fairly plausible. For although an irrational person could probably will amost anything, it surely would be difficult for a perfectly rational person to will that something be a law of nature if that thing could not be a law of nature. Let us grant, then, that it would not be possible for the agent to consistently will that $GM(a_1)$ be a law of nature if in fact $GM(a_1)$ could not be a law of nature.

The first premise is the most troublesome. Kant apparently assumes that "self-love" has as its function, the stimulation of the furtherance of life. Given this, he seems to reason that self-love cannot also contribute sometimes to the destruction of life. Perhaps Kant assumes that a given feeling cannot have two "opposite" functions. However, if $GM(a_1)$ were a law of nature, self-love would have to contribute toward self-destruction in some cases. Hence, Kant seems to conclude, $GM(a_1)$ cannot be a law of nature. And so we have our first premise.

If this is Kant's reasoning, it is not very impressive. In the first place, it is not clear why we should suppose that self-love has the function of stimulating the furtherance of life. Indeed, it is not clear why we should suppose that self-love has any function at all! Second, it is hard to see why self-love can't serve two "opposite" functions. Perhaps self-love motivates us to stay alive when continued life would be pleasant, but motivates us to stop living when continued life would be unpleasant. Why should we hold this to be impossible?

So it appears that Kant's first illustration is not entirely successful. Before we turn to the second illustration, however, a few further comments may be in order. First, some philosophers would say that it is better that Kant's argument failed here. Many moralists would take the following position: Kant's view about suicide is wrong. The act of suicide out of self-love, a_1, is morally blameless. In certain circumstances suicide is each person's "own business." Thus, these moralists would say that if the categorical imperative did imply that a_1 is morally wrong, as Kant tries to show, then Kant's theory would be defective. But since Kant was not entirely successful in showing that his theory had this implication, the theory has not been shown to have any incorrect results.

A second point to notice about the suicide example is its scope. It is important to recognize that in this passage Kant has not attempted to show that suicide is always wrong. Perhaps Kant's personal view is that it is never right to commit suicide. However, in the passage in question he attempts to show only that a certain act of suicide, one based on a certain maxim, would be wrong. For all Kant has said here, other acts of suicide, done according to other maxims, might be permitted by the categorical imperative.

Let us turn now to the second illustration. Suppose I find myself hard-pressed financially and I decide that the only way in which I can get some money is by borrowing it from a friend. I realize that I will have to promise to repay the money, even though I won't in fact be able to do so. For I foresee that my financial situation will be even worse later on than it is at present. If I perform this action, a_2, of borrowing money on a false promise, I will perform it on this maxim:

$M(a_2)$: When I need money and can get some by borrowing it on a false promise, then I shall borrow the money and promise to repay, even though I know that I won't be able to repay.

The generalized form of my maxim is this:

$GM(a_2)$: Whenever anyone needs money and can get some by borrowing it on a false promise, then he will borrow the money and promise to repay, even though he knows that he won't be able to repay.

Kant's view is that I cannot consistently will that GM(a$_2$) be a law of nature. This view emerges clearly in the following passage:

> . . . I can by no means will a universal law of lying; for by such a law there could properly be no promises at all, since it would be futile to profess a will for future action to others who would not believe my profession or who, if they did so over-hastily, would pay me back in like coin; and consequently my maxim, as soon as it was made a universal law, would be bound to annual itself.[15]

It is important to be clear about what Kant is saying here. He is not arguing against lying on the grounds that if I lie, others will soon lose confidence in me and eventually won't believe my promises. Nor is he arguing against lying on the grounds that my lie will contribute to a general practice of lying, which in turn will lead to a breakdown of trust and the destruction of the practice of promising. These considerations are basically utilitarian. Kant's point is more subtle. He is saying that there is something covertly self-contradictory about the state of affairs in which, as a law of nature, everyone makes a false promise when in need of a loan. Perhaps Kant's point is this: Such a state of affairs is self-contradictory because, on the one hand, in such a state of affairs everyone in need would borrow money on a false promise, and yet, on the other hand, in that state of affairs no one could borrow money on a false promise—for if promises were always violated, who would be silly enough to loan any money?

Since the state of affairs in which everyone in need borrows money on a false promise is covertly self-contradictory, it is irrational to will it to occur. No one can consistently will that this state of affairs should occur. But for me to will that GM(a$_2$) be a law of nature is just for me to will that this impossible state of affairs occur. Hence, I cannot consistently will that the generalized form of my maxim be a law of nature. According to CI$_1$, my act is not right unless I can consistently will that the generalized form of its maxim be a law of nature. Hence, according to CI$_1$, my act of borrowing the money on the false promise is not morally right.

---

[15]*Ibid.*, p. 71.

We can restate the essentials of this argument much more succinctly:

Lying-Promise Example

(1) $GM(a_2)$ cannot be a law of nature.
(2) If $GM(a_2)$ cannot be a law of nature, then I cannot consistently will that $GM(a_2)$ be a law of nature.
(3) a_2 is morally right if and only if I can consistently will that $GM(a_2)$ be a law of nature.
(4) Therefore, a_2 is not morally right.

The first premise is based upon the view that it would somehow be self-contradictory for it to be a law of nature that everyone in need makes a lying promise. For in that (allegedly impossible) state of affairs there would be promises, since those in need would make them, and there would also not be promises, since no one would believe that anyone was really committing himself to future payment by the use of the words "I promise." So, as Kant says, the generalized form of the maxim "annuls itself." It cannot be a law of nature.

The second premise is just like the second premise in the previous example. It is based on the idea that it is somehow irrational to will that something be the case if in fact it is impossible for it to be the case. So if it really is impossible for $GM(a_2)$ to be a law of nature, then it would be irrational of me to will that it be so. Hence, I cannot consistently will that the generalized form of my maxim be a law of nature. In other words, I cannot consistently will that it be a law of nature that whenever anyone needs money and can get some on a false promise, then he will borrow some and promise to repay, even though he knows he won't be able to repay.

The third premise of the argument is the categorical imperative. If the rest of the argument is acceptable, then the argument as a whole shows that the categorical imperative, together with these other facts, implies that my lying promise would not be morally right. This would seem to be a reasonable result.

Some readers have apparently taken this example to show that according to Kantianism, it is always wrong to make a false promise. Indeed, Kant himself may have come to this conclusion. Yet if we reflect on the argument for a moment, we will see that the view of these readers is surely not the case. At best, the argument shows only that one specific act of making a false promise would be wrong. That one act is judged to be wrong because its maxim allegedly cannot be universalized. Other acts of making false promises would have to be evaluated independently. Perhaps it will turn out that every act of making a false promise has a maxim that cannot be universalized. If so, CI_1 would imply that they are all wrong. So far, however, we have been given no reason to suppose that this is the case.

Other critics would insist that Kant hasn't even succeeded in showing that a_2 is morally wrong. They would claim that the first premise of the argument is false. Surely it could be a law of nature that everyone will make a false promise when in need of money, they would say. If people borrowed money on false promises rarely enough, and kept their word on other promises, then no contradiction would arise. There would then be no reason to suppose that "no one would believe he was being promised anything, but would laugh at utterances of this kind as empty shams."[16]

Let us turn, then, to the third example. Kant now illustrates the application of the categorical imperative to a case of imperfect duty to oneself. The action in question is the "neglect of natural talents." Kant apparently holds that it is wrong for a person to let all of his natural talents go to waste. Of course, if a person has several natural talents, he is not required to develop all of them. Perhaps Kant considers this to be an imperfect duty partly because a person has the freedom to select which talents he will develop and which he will allow to rust.

Kant imagines the case of someone who is comfortable as he is and who, out of laziness, contemplates performing the act, a_3, of letting all his talents rust. His maxim in doing this would be:

$M(a_3)$: When I am comfortable as I am, I shall let my talents rust.

When generalized, the maxim becomes:

$GM(a_3)$: Whenever anyone is comfortable as he is, he will let his talents rust.

Kant admits that $GM(a_3)$ could be a law of nature. Thus, his argument in this case differs from the arguments he produced in the

---

[16]*Ibid.*

first two cases. Kant proceeds to outline the reasoning by which the agent would come to see that it would be wrong to perform a_3:

> He then sees that a system of nature could indeed always subsist under such a universal law, although (like the South Sea Islanders) every man should let his talents rust and should be bent on devoting his life solely to idleness, indulgence, procreation, and, in a word, to enjoyment. Only he cannot possibly *will* that this should become a universal law of nature or should be implanted in us as such a law by a natural instinct. For as a rational being he necessarily wills that all his powers should be developed, since they serve him, and are given him for all sorts of possible ends.[17]

Once again, Kant's argument seems to be based on a rather dubious appeal to natural purposes. Allegedly, nature implanted our talents in us for all sorts of purposes. Hence, we necessarily will to develop them. If we also will to let them rust, we are willing both to develop them (as we must) and to refrain from developing them. Anyone who wills both of these things obviously wills inconsistently. Hence, the agent cannot consistently will that his talents rust. This, together with the categorical imperative, implies that it would be wrong to perform the act, a_3, of letting one's talents rust.

The argument can be put as follows:

Rusting-Talents Example

(1) Everyone necessarily wills that all his talents be developed.

(2) If everyone necessarily wills that all his talents be developed, then the agent of a_3 cannot consistently will that $GM(a_3)$ be a law of nature.

(3) a_3 is morally right if and only if the agent of a_3 can consistently will that $GM(a_3)$ be a law of nature.

(4) Therefore a_3 is not morally right.

This argument seems even less persuasive than the others. In the quoted passage Kant himself presents a counterexample to the first premise. The South Sea Islanders, according to Kant, do not will to

---

[17]*Ibid.*

develop their talents. This fact, if it is one, is surely inconsistent with the claim that we all necessarily will that all our talents be developed. Even if Kant is wrong about the South Sea Islanders, his first premise is still extremely implausible. Couldn't there be a rational person who, out of idleness, simply does not will to develop his talents? If there could not be such a person, then what is the point of trying to show that we are under some specifically moral obligation to develop all our talents?

Once again, however, some philosophers may feel that Kant would have been worse off if his example had succeeded. These philosophers would hold that we in fact have no moral obligation to develop our talents. If Kant's theory had entailed that we have such an obligation, they would insist, then that would have shown that Kant's theory is defective.

In Kant's fourth illustration the categorical imperative is applied to an imperfect duty to others—the duty to help others who are in distress. Kant describes a man who is flourishing and who contemplates performing the act, a_4, of giving nothing to charity. His maxim is not stated by Kant in this passage, but it can probably be formulated as follows:

$M(a_4)$: When I'm flourishing and others are in distress, I shall give nothing to charity.

When generalized, this maxim becomes:

$GM(a_4)$: Whenever anyone is flourishing and others are in distress, he will give nothing to charity.

As in the other example of imperfect duty, Kant acknowledges that $GM(a_4)$ could be a law of nature. Yet he claims once again that the agent cannot consistently will that it be a law of nature. He explains this by arguing as follows:

> For a will which decided in this way would be in conflict with itself, since many a situation might arise in which the man needed love and sympathy from others, and in which, by such a law of nature sprung from his own will, he would rob himself of all hope of the help he wants for himself.[18]

---

[18]*Ibid.*, p. 91.

Kant's point here seems to be this: The day may come when the agent is no longer flourishing. He may need charity from others. If that day does come, then he will find that he wills that others give him such aid. However, in willing that $GM(a_4)$ be a law of nature, he has already willed that no one should give charitable aid to anyone. Hence, on that dark day, his will will contradict itself. Thus, he cannot consistently will that $GM(a_4)$ be a law of nature. This being so, the categorical imperative entails that a_4 is not right.

If this is Kant's reasoning, then his reasoning is defective. For we cannot infer from the fact that the person *may* someday want aid from others, that he in fact already is willing inconsistently when he wills today that no one should give aid to anyone. The main reason for this is that that dark day may not come, in which case no conflict will arise. Furthermore, as is pretty obvious upon reflection, even if that dark day does arrive, the agent may steadfastly stick to his general policy. He may say, "I didn't help others when they were in need, and now that I'm in need I don't want any help from them." In this way, he would avoid having inconsistent policies. Unless this attitude is irrational, which it does not seem to be, Kant's fourth example is unsuccessful. . . .

In light of the conclusions reached [thus far], it may seem that Kant's categorical imperative is unacceptable as a moral theory. So far, however, we have considered only the first formulation of the categorical imperative. Kant presents several other principles, each of which he says is a formulation of the same doctrine. Perhaps when Kant says that these other principles are formulations of the same doctrine, what he means is that each of these other principles is extensionally equivalent to CI_1. In any case, we should look into these other versions of the categorical imperative to see whether we can find in any of them a more plausible moral theory.

The Formula of the End in Itself

We draw a broad distinction between things that are good as means, and things that are good as ends. The distinction emerges clearly enough if we select some good thing and ask why it is good. Take sunlight. Sunlight is surely a good thing. But why is it good? Some would say that sunlight is good because, among other things, it makes plants grow, and it is a good thing that plants grow. But why is it good that plants grow? It is good that plants grow, it could be maintained, because without plants there would be no life on the earth, and it is good that there is life. But why is it good that there is life? Life, many would say, is good in itself. Its goodness does not arise as a result of what it leads to, or contributes to. It is good not because of its results, but because of itself. If these reflections about life are correct, then we can say that sunlight is good as a *means*, whereas life is good as an *end*. Another way to put this would be to say that sunlight is extrinsically good, whereas life is intrinsically good. Still another way to put it would be to say that sunlight is a means, whereas life is an end in itself.

We can define "means" in terms of "end in itself":

D_1: x is a means = df. there is something, y, that is an end in itself, and x contributes, directly or indirectly, to the existence of y.

Thus, according to D_1, sunlight is a means, since it contributes to the existence of life, which we are assuming to be an end in itself. If life is an end in itself, then money, health, education, and abundant natural resources may be taken to be good as means. Each of these things contributes to life, something that may be good in itself.

Philosophers have disagreed about what in fact is an end in itself. Mill and others have said that pleasure is the only thing that is an end in itself. G. E. Moore claimed that the love of beauty is an end in itself. Others have said that knowledge, virtue, and pleasure are all ends in themselves. Perhaps we would not go too far wrong if we said, following Moore, that a thing is an end in itself if and only if it would still be good even if it existed in complete isolation.

Kant claims that "rational nature exists as an end in itself."[19] By this, he seems to mean that all rational beings, including people, are ends in themselves. In other words, every person is intrinsically good. From this, Kant infers that it can never be morally right to treat any person merely as a means. That is, it is never morally right to treat a person as if he were simply a useful object for your own purposes. This view, which is the second version of the categorical imperative, is stated by Kant in a variety of ways:

---

[19]*Ibid.*, p. 96.

> Act in such a way that you always treat humanity, whether in your own person or in the person of any other, never simply as a means, but always at the same time as an end.[20]
>
> A rational being, by his very nature an end and consequently an end in himself, must serve for every maxim as a condition limiting all merely relative and arbitrary ends.[21]
>
> So act in relation to every rational being (both to yourself and to others) that he may at the same time count in your maxim as an end in himself.[22]

Let us understand Kant to be saying in these passages that one ought never to act in such a way as to treat anyone merely as a means. In other words:

> CI_2: An act is morally right if and only if the agent, in performing it, refrains from treating any person merely as a means.

According to CI_2, there is a moral prohibition against treating anyone merely as a means. We should recognize that CI_2 does not rule out treating a person as a means. That is, CI_2 must not be confused with this rather implausible view:

> CI_2': An act is morally right if and only if, in performing it, the agent refrains from treating any person as a means.

CI_2' rules out any act in which the agent treats anyone as a means. But this is absurd, since we use other people as means to our ends all the time, and we cannot avoid doing so. A student uses his teacher as a means to gaining an education; a teacher uses her students as a means to gaining a livelihood; a customer in a restaurant uses his waiter as a means to gaining his dinner. None of these acts is ruled out by CI_2. For in each of these cases the agent of the act may also treat the others involved, *at least in part*, as ends in themselves. Thus, although these acts would violate a preposterous principle such as CI_2', it is not clear that they would have to violate the more plausible principle, CI_2. For as we are understanding it,

---

[20]*Ibid.*

[21]*Ibid.*, p. 104.

[22]*Ibid.*, p. 105.

this second version of the categorical imperative only rules out treating persons *merely* as means.

CI_2 embodies an important moral insight, one that many would find plausible. It is the idea that it is wrong to "use" people. People are not mere objects, to be manipulated to serve our purpose. We cannot treat people as we treat wrecked cars, or wilted flowers, or old tin cans. Such things can be thrown out or destroyed when we no longer have any use for them. People, on the other hand, have dignity and worth, and must be treated accordingly.

Thus, what CI_2 says seems fairly plausible. Nevertheless, many moral philosophers would be uneasy about the claim that CI_2 is a formulation of "the supreme principle of morality." Can it really be the case that *all* wrong action is action in which people are used merely as means? Can all of our moral obligations be seen as obligations to treat people as ends? Some philosophers, admitting that it is important to treat people with respect, will deny that CI_2 captures the whole of our moral obligation. Others may even have their doubts about the acceptability of the insight embodied in CI_2, even if that insight were interpreted rather generously. Thus, it would be useful to see why Kant thinks CI_2 is true.

An Argument for CI_2

Kant suggests what seems to be a fairly interesting argument for CI_2. First, he points out that if there is something that is good as an end in itself, then that thing will provide a "ground of a possible categorical imperative."[23] By this, Kant seems to mean that if there is something that is good as an end in itself, then there is a true moral principle to the effect that this thing, whatever it may be, ought to be treated as if it were good as an end in itself. This seems reasonable.

Then Kant tries to show that people are ends in themselves. If he can succeed in establishing this point, then he will have a simple argument to show that people ought to be treated as ends in themselves. From this, it is not a very great step to the conclusion that an act is morally right if and only if the agent, in performing it, refrains from treating any person merely as a means.

---

[23]*Ibid.*, p. 95.

Kant's argument that people exist as ends in themselves is rather complex, but the main thrust of it appears in the following passage:

> Persons . . . are not merely subjective ends whose existence as an object of our actions has a value *for us*: they are *objective ends*—that is, things whose existence is in itself an end, and indeed an end such that in its place we can put no other end to which they should serve *simply* as means; for unless this is so, nothing at all of *absolute* value would be found anywhere. But if all value were conditioned—that is, contingent—then no supreme principle could be found for reason at all.[24]

We can simplify what appears to be Kant's argument as follows:

People-Are-Ends Argument

(1) If people are not ends in themselves, then nothing is an end in itself.

(2) If nothing is an end in itself, then there is never any reason to act in one way rather than in any other.

(3) There is sometimes a reason to act in one way rather than in another.

(4) Therefore, people are ends in themselves.

In this form, the argument is valid. Furthermore, at least two of the premises seem quite plausible. The second premise asserts that if nothing is an end, then no act is preferable to any other. This may seem odd, but it makes sense. To see why, consider, if you can, a state of affairs in which nothing is an end in itself. If there is nothing that is an end in itself, then there is nothing that is a means. For according to D_1, to say that something, x, is a means is just to say that there is some end in itself, y, such that x contributes to the existence of y. With no end, there can be no means. Thus, if there is nothing good as an end in itself, then there is nothing good either as an end or as a means. Hence, in these circumstances there would be nothing good at all. But if nothing is good at all, there can be no good reason to prefer any action to any other action. In this way, we can see that if there is nothing good as an end, then there is no reason to act in one way rather than in any other. This establishes (2).

---

[24]*Ibid.*, p. 96.

Premise (3) is pretty straightforward. If we grant that some alternatives are morally preferable to others, then we must grant (3). The only person who would deny (3) is one who rejects morality altogether. Surely, the views of such a person may be ignored here.

Thus, the whole argument seems to turn on premise (1). It is clear that Kant affirms (1). He explicitly says that people are "objective ends," and he goes on to say that "unless this is so, nothing at all of absolute value will be found anywhere."[25] Yet it is not easy to see why Kant maintains this view. Isn't it possible that people are not ends in themselves, but that pleasure, for example, is? Some moralists would deny that people are ends in themselves, but would maintain that beautiful objects are ends in themselves. Others would say that people are good only as means, since the things that are good as ends are one and all mental states that exist only if there are people. In order to establish (1), Kant has to show that all such views are mistaken. He has to show that if people are not intrinsically good, then nothing is. Without some persuasive argument, it is not easy to accept this premise.

So Kant's argument is rather weak. He hasn't shown that people are ends in themselves. Nevertheless, many people would agree with Kant on this point. They would say that whether it can be proved or not, people are in fact ends in themselves. If this view is correct, it would of course be reasonable to maintain that people ought to be treated with the respect and consideration due to things of such great value.

Problems for CI$_2$

The greatest problem for CI$_2$ is not, however, the lack of a convincing proof. Nor is it that CI$_2$ is subject to obvious counterexamples. Rather, the main difficulty with CI$_2$ is that its meaning is never made sufficiently clear. The most troublesome concept in this version of the categorical imperative is the concept of "treating someone merely as a means." It is pretty clear that if you own and mistreat slaves, then you treat them as means. But what about some more typical cases? What about a patron in a diner who grunts out his order to the waitress without even looking at her?

---

[25]*Ibid.*

What about a "freeloader" who lives with relatives? What about a factory owner who pays minimum wages and refuses to install safety equipment? Are these people treating others merely as means? Suppose the patron smiles and leaves a tip. Suppose the freeloader offers to do some work around the house. Suppose the factory owner gives a bonus at Christmas. Would they still be treating others merely as means? Would they be treating them, in part, as ends in themselves? It is very hard to tell. . . .

Conclusion

Kant's moral philosophy thus turns out to have some merits and some very great defects. Its merits are fairly clear. Kant has gathered together and defended a variety of extremely important moral insights. Upon examination, many of our deepest moral convictions will be found to rest upon these insights. Let us attempt to state some of these views.

Many of us would agree with Kant that there is something objectionable about a person who acts in a way in which he would not want others to act. A person who takes advantage of the forbearance of others, and thereby makes himself an exception to a rule he endorsed for them, is an immoral person. This view, not adequately accounted for by the utilitarians, would strike many moralists as being essential to any adequate moral theory. Kant's first formulation of the categorical imperative seems to be an attempt to capture this view.

Another widely accepted doctrine is that in all our actions we must recognize the great intrinsic value of human life. Murder, slavery, and other forms of "using people" elicit our strongest moral disapproval. People are not merely things to be manipulated for one's personal ends. People are to be treated with respect. Kant's second formulation of the categorical imperative seems to be an attempt to capture this view. . . .

The great defect of Kant's moral philosophy is that he failed to develop any of these intuitions adequately. His presentation is so complex, his terminology so obscure, and his argument so confused that the careful reader is rarely confident that he knows precisely what Kant wants to say, or why he wants to say it. Even in our brief survey of some of Kant's most basic arguments and doctrines, we have found time and time again that his meaning is obscure. Unfortunately, with respect to many of these arguments and doctrines, it is very hard to develop a clear interpretation that is both plausible and recognizably Kantian in spirit. If we assume that moral philosophy is, among other things, an attempt to discover, clarify, and defend the truth about ethics, then we must conclude that Kant's work in moral philosophy, though extraordinarily rich and suggestive, is not entirely successful.

Respect for Persons and Fraternity

R. S. PETERS

Richard Peters (b. 1919) is a professor of philosophy and education at the University of London. He is the author of several books, including *Ethics and Education* and *Authority, Responsibility, and Education*.

Peters's article seeks to show how human rationality entails attitudes of fraternity and respect for persons. He begins with Kant's idea that what we respect in a person is the authority of the moral laws that govern how we may behave to him or her. Yet, says Peters, this doctrine seems too impersonal. Someone can act in a principled way to another whom he or she despises. Peters therefore seeks to show that this is to misunderstand how Kant sees the relation between dignity and the moral law. The moral law, as Kant understood it, is a creation of autonomous rational beings. "Kant's conception of law was therefore inseparable from his belief in the activity, dignity, and worth of rational individuals who created it." Peters develops this idea in his own way, laying

RESPECT FOR PERSONS AND FRATERNITY From *Ethics and Education* by R. S. Peters. Reprinted by permission of George Allen & Unwin (Publishers) Ltd.

stress on individual autonomy. Each person is a "center of valuation," he says; to respect a person is therefore to be considerate of that person's special point of view. In this way Peters develops Kant's seemingly impersonal idea of respect in a more personal direction.

What has to be shown . . . from the point of view of ethical theory in general . . . is that there are some attitudes towards others that a rational man must have. The case, therefore, for respect for persons and for fraternity must now be presented.

Respect for Persons

Kant held that respect for persons was derivative from respect for law. He argued that though respect is a feeling, it is not a feeling received through influence, but is

> *self-wrought* by a rational concept, and, therefore, is specifically distinct from all feelings of the former kind, which may be referred either to inclination or fear. What I recognize immediately as a law for me, I recognize with respect. . . . The *object* of respect is the *law* only, that is, the law which we impose on *ourselves*, and yet recognize as necessary in itself. . . . Respect for a person is properly only respect for the law (of honesty, etc.) of which he gives us an example.

The difficulty about this view is that contempt for persons seems, prima facie at any rate, quite compatible with meticulousness in acting on principles. One could take careful account of a person's interests, for instance, as a guardian might that of his ward, and yet have and show contempt for him as a person. It does not look, therefore, as if the appraisal which goes with respect for law or principles necessarily either coincides with or implies that which is necessary for respect for persons.

Kant, however, had a distinctive concept of law, at least in the practical sphere, in that for him the thought of such laws was inseparable from that of the autonomous rational beings who created them. The principles of practical reason were not "out there" to discover; they were not, as in Plato's system, principles permeating the nature of things which a rational being might discern; they were the creation of individuals possessed of reason and desire. Kant's conception of law was therefore inseparable from his belief in the activity, dignity, and worth of rational individuals who created it. For him the existence of individual rational beings was not just a fact about the world; it was a fact of supreme ethical importance. The notion of "persons" picked out not simply the fact; it also bore witness to the ethical importance of the fact. And this fact was intimately connected with the activity of men as rational beings in deliberating about what they ought to do.

The Meaning of "Respect for Persons"

There is much to be said for this doctrine of Kant in that the notion of being a person is connected with "being on the inside" of those experiences which are characteristic of practical reason, of acting on principles, and of determining the future in the light of knowledge of the past and awareness of what may be. Choice, which is intimately connected with the exercise of practical reason, is too narrow a concept; for it implies deliberation between alternatives. It does not cover such things as the grasp of rules, the formulation and statement of intentions, and the making of promises by means of which individuals determine the future. Notions like that of "endeavor" used by Spinoza to characterize a general tendency to persist in a form of being are too general; for they apply also to plants and other homeostatic systems which are not conscious of themselves or of the past and future. The notion is much more that of an assertive point of view; of judgments, appraisals, intentions, and decisions that shape events, their characteristic stamp being determined by previous ones that have given rise to permanent or semi-permanent dispositions. The shaping of a pattern of life in this way is constitutive of what we call an individual person. When it is said that a man who brainwashes others, or who settles their lives for them without consulting them shows lack of "respect for persons," the implication is that he does not treat others seriously as agents or as determiners of their own destiny, and that he disregards their feelings and view of the world. He either refuses to let them be in a situation where their intentions, decisions, appraisals, and choices can operate effectively, or he purposely interferes with or nullifies their capacity for self-direction. He ensures that for them the question "What ought I to do?" either scarcely arises or serves as a cork on a tide of events whose drift derives from elsewhere. He denies them the dignity which is the due of a self-determining agent who is capable of valuation and choice and who has a point of view of his own about his own future and interests.

The notion of a "person," which is picked out by reference to such notions connected with being an assertive point of view, is narrower than the wider notion of being an "individual." For instance, the individual's awareness of pain, or his visual experience, is not necessarily a manifestation of his existence as a person; if it were so dogs and octopuses would be persons. Yet the principle of consideration of interests could be applied to dogs without ever treating them as persons. A policy would have to be pursued which took account of avoiding pain for them and maximizing their opportunities for satisfaction. This would be done without "respect for persons"; for the dog's point of view about his forms of satisfaction would not be taken into account.

It is possible, too, for individual men and women to live together in society without any clear consciousness of themselves as persons. They might be thought of as having claims or interests, as occupying a certain status; but their view of such matters as individuals might be totally disregarded. Societies are really nothing more than groups of individuals who are initiated into and who accept and maintain a public system of rules. Nevertheless it is quite possible for people to live in societies without any awareness of the determining role of individuals. Indeed they may not distinguish clearly between a social order and a natural order and may think that individual men are comparatively impotent in relation to both of them. Though we might say that they were potentially individual persons who had been conditioned to accept a rather womb-like existence, they might nevertheless have no consciousness of themselves as persons. They might be conscious only of their particular social roles and of their general kinship with other members of the society. They might have neither respect for persons nor consciousness of either themselves or others as persons in any important sense.

People only begin to think of themselves as persons, centers of valuation, decision, and choice, in so far as the fact that conscious-ness is individuated into distinct centers, linked with distinct physical bodies and with distinctive points of view, is taken to be a matter of importance in a society. And they will only really develop as persons in so far as they learn to think of themselves as such. The concept of being a person, in other words, is derivative from the valuation placed in a society upon the determining role of indi-vidual points of view. Individuals will only tend to assert their rights as individuals, to take pride in their achievements, to deliber-ate carefully and choose "for themselves" what they ought to do, and to develop their own individual style of emotional reaction—in other words they will only tend to manifest all the various prop-erties which we associate with being "persons"—if they are en-couraged to do so. They would be persons all right in the sense that the moral laws were true in virtue of which they had such rights; but if such rights were not recognized they would not be treated as persons, would not think of themselves as such. Even in a society which, because of the importance which it attaches to individual points of view, is permeated by the concept of a person, an indi-vidual who was systematically discouraged and sat on might have such a low opinion of himself that we might be inclined to say of him that he simply had not got the concept of himself "as a person." What we might mean is that he had the concept of a person but that, because of special circumstances, he was incapable of applying it to himself. Presumably, at certain periods, slaves have been in just this predicament.

In our society being a person matters very much. Individuals are encouraged to judge and choose things "for themselves"; they are held responsible for the consequences of their actions as individuals and are praised and blamed accordingly; they feel pride for things well done and guilt and remorse for things badly done. They are encouraged to be the determiners of their own destiny and, to a certain extent, they *are* so because our society encourages this form of individual assertion. This consciousness of being an individual person rather than just a member of a group is therefore both exhilarating and sobering. The sense of mastery and making an impact on the shape of things is mingled with apprehension for the consequences of failure. Men, however, come to value it very much for what there is in it, as distinct from the value attached to it

47

by their society. Indeed were it not the case that there is much in it to prize, it is difficult to see how societies would come to attach such overriding value to the assertion of an individual point of view.

This consciousness of being a person reaches its zenith, perhaps, in the experience of entering into and sustaining a personal relationship which is based on reciprocal agreement, where the bonds that bind people together derive from their own appraisals and choice, not from any status or institutional position. They create their own world by voluntarily sharing together and mingling their own individual perspectives on and developments of the public life of their society. The obligations, mainly of a contractual nature, which sustain their relationship are felt to be more binding than most duties simply because they are explicitly undertaken and because they create pools of predictability in a realm which was previously subject only to the play of natural appetites and aversions within a world marked out by impersonal traditions and institutional pressures.

A person who is conscious of his own agency in shaping events is also aware of the irksomeness of external forces that may prevent or impede him in doing what he wants. He has learned, however, to come to terms with the confines of nature; for his concept of himself as an agent develops *pari passu* with the concept of a nature which is unaffected by human whims and wishes. It is only in the autistic thinking of the infant, or in magic, that the natural world is subject to human whims and wishes. But he is vividly aware of the irksomeness of constraints imposed on him by other men; for he knows that these are alterable and often unnecessary, as well as frustrating to his purposes. But more irksome of all is the refusal by others to let him determine his own destiny and order his own preference in any major respect by conceiving of goals, deliberating about alternatives, and attempting to implement those of his choosing. To be treated as a moron or merely as an instrument of the purposes of other men, and to have his feelings completely disregarded is intolerable for a man who is conscious of his own potentialities as self-determining agent. It may not be so, of course, for a man who has always been a slave and who has no consciousness of what he might achieve as an agent; there is no reason to suppose that slaves were discontented with their lot as long as they viewed their situation as part of the order of things.

The Question of Justification

It has been argued that in so far as a man has the concept of himself and of others as persons, he must have been initiated into a society in which there is a general norm which attaches importance to the assertive points of view emanating from individual centers of consciousness. A man develops as a person as this concept of himself and of others develops. He also comes to value what is involved in being a person for what there is in it, as distinct from the importance attached to it by the social norm. To ask him, therefore, whether persons ought to be respected is rather like asking a man whether he ought to be afraid of a dangerous situation; for the concept of respect is necessary to explicate what is meant by a person. If he has the concept of person and understands it fully from "the inside" (i.e., not just as an anthropologist might "understand," or fail to understand, a concept purely on the basis of external observation), then he must also have the notion that it matters that individuals represent distinct assertive points of view.

The explication of a concept, however, never settles a question of policy. The problem is to produce an argument to establish that any rational being must have the concept of a person and therefore respect others and himself as such. The procedure must therefore be to return to the situation of practical reason and to show that respect for persons is a presupposition that any participant in such a situation must accept. An argument must be advanced to show that it would be impossible for a man to take part seriously in the situation of practical reason who lacked this basic attitude to his fellow participants.

Such an argument is not far to seek. Indeed it has been implicit, as would be expected, if the lines of the analysis of "person" are correct, in the various characterizations of what it means to be a person. Central among these are experiences connected with the individual being the determiner of his own destiny, and with representing an assertive point of view. These phrases are attempts to intimate the sort of presuppositions that any man must have about himself and about others if he is to enter into any rational discussion with them about what ought to be done. . . . Any man entering such a discussion seriously must claim freedom from interference for doing what there are reasons for doing and must assume that consideration must be accorded to him in so far as he has interests

49

whose nature he wants to determine. If he was going to be subject to arbitrary interference, and if no prima facie attention was going to be paid to his assessment of his interests, such a discussion would lack any point. He must presume, too, that what holds for himself holds also for any other man who seriously joins with him in trying to answer such questions. Within such a discussion, too, the principle of impartiality requires that he listen to what people say and assent to or dissent from their contributions according to relevant criteria, *e.g.*, the quality of arguments adduced, and ignore irrelevant considerations such as the color of the eyes or hair of the contributors. These general principles governing the situation of practical reason are precisely those which safeguard the experiences which we most intimately associate with being a person, i.e., not being arbitrarily interfered with in respect of the execution of our wants and decisions and not having our claims and interests ignored or treated in a partial or prejudiced manner. . . .

If may be found, of course, that particular people are inarticulate or stupid, or that they are dishonest in the manner in which they advance claims. All such factors are relevant to the attention paid to particular people on particular occassions. But the argument is not meant to show that anyone must do anything particular on any particular occasions. Rather it relates to prima facie principles which a man must *in general* accept if he is determined to settle things, in so far as he can, by discussion.

The norm of respect for persons, therefore, picks out as crucial those types of experience, which are a selection from the more varied range of experiences located at an individual center of consciousness, which are of cardinal importance for those entering seriously into discussion with their fellows about courses of action or ways of living. "Respect for persons" is therefore a principle which summarizes the attitude which we must adopt towards others with whom we are prepared seriously to discuss what ought to be done. Their point of view must be taken into account as sources of claims and interests; they must be regarded as having a prima facie claim for noninterference in doing what is in their interest; and no arbitrariness must be shown towards them as participants in discussion. To have the concept of a person is to see an individual as an object of respect in a form of life which is conducted on the basis of those principles which are presuppositions of the use of practical reason. . . .

What If Everyone Did That?

COLIN STRANG

Colin Strang (b. 1922) is a reader in philosophy at the University of Newcastle-upon-Tyne. He writes in the areas of ethics and Greek philosophy.

An individual who refrains from voting or evades taxes or conscription is often charged with wrongdoing. In part the reason for calling such evasion wrong is the disastrous consequences that would ensue if everyone were to do the same. To this the evader sometimes replies, "But in fact not everyone will do the same." Since some will act and some will not, the evader asks, "Why me?" One rejoinder to this is, "Why not you?" Strang carefully examines the pros and cons of the exchange, and he shows that the question "Why not you?" has greater force.

I want to discuss the force and validity of the familiar type of ethical argument epitomized in my title. A typical example of it would be: "If everyone refrained from voting the result would be disastrous, therefore *you* ought to vote." Now since the argument is addressed to the person concerned simply *qua* member of the class of people entitled to vote, it could be addressed with equal force to any

WHAT IF EVERYONE DID THAT? From *Durham University Journal*, 53 (1960). Reprinted by permission of the author and the publisher.

member or all members of that class indifferently; so that conclusion might just as validly be: "therefore *everyone* ought to vote."

There is no doubt that this argument has some force. People *are* sometimes impressed by it. But it is not nearly so obvious that it is a valid one, that is, that they *ought* to be impressed by it.

One way of not being impressed by it is to reply: "Yes, but everyone *won't* refrain from voting, so there will be no disaster, so it's all right for me not to vote." But this reply is beside the point. The argument never claimed that this one abstention would lead to disaster, nor did it claim that universal abstention (which *would* be disastrous) would occur; indeed it implied, on each point, the very opposite. This brings out the important fact that the argument does not appeal to the consequences of the action it condemns and so is not of a utilitarian type, but that it is applicable, if anywhere, just where utilitarian arguments do *not* apply.

The objector, who remains unimpressed, will continue: "Granted that my first objection is beside the point, I still can't see how you get from your premiss to your conclusion. Your premiss is, roughly: 'Everyone's nonvoting is to be deplored,' and your conclusion is: 'Everyone's voting is obligatory.' Why should it be irrational to accept the premiss but deny the conclusion? In any case the validity of the argument cannot depend on its form alone. Plenty of arguments of the very same form are plainly invalid. For instance; if everyone switched on their electric fires at 9 a.m. sharp there would be a power breakdown, therefore no one should; furthermore, this argument applies not only to 9 a.m. but to all times, so no one should ever switch on an electric fire. Again, if everyone taught philosophy whole-time we should all starve, so no one should; or if everyone built houses or did anything else whatever (bar farming) whole-time, we should all starve; and if everyone farmed we would be without clothes or shelter and would die of exposure in winter, so no one should farm. It rather looks, on your kind of argument, as if every whole-time activity is forbidden to everyone. Conversely, if no one farmed we would all starve, so everyone should farm; if no one made clothes we would all die of exposure, so everyone ought to make clothes—and so on. So it also looks, on your kind of argument, as if all sorts of part-time activity are obligatory on everybody. You surely do not mean to commit yourself to enjoining self-sufficiency and condemning specialization? What I want to know is why some arguments of this form are valid (as you claim) while others are not (as you must admit)." . . .

Compare the voting case with this one: "If everyone here refuses to dig a latrine the camp will be insanitary, therefore everyone ought to dig one." Surely the conclusion we want is, rather: "therefore *someone* ought to dig one." In the voting case, on the other hand, given the premiss "If everyone refused to vote there would be no government," the conclusion "therefore someone ought to vote" clearly will not do; and even the conclusion "therefore everyone ought to vote" is hardly cogent on the reasonable assumption that a 10 per cent abstention will do no harm. If the argument is to be at all cogent it must make some reference to the percentage vote (say n%) needed, thus: "If more than $(100 - n)$ per cent of the electorate abstained there would be no government"; this allows us to draw an acceptable conclusion, that is, "therefore n per cent must vote to avert anarchy and one must dig to avert disease. But our argument has gained in cogency and precision (being now of a simple utilitarian kind) only at the expense of being no longer effective, or even seemingly so, against the defaulter. He will reply: "All right, so n per cent ought to vote (someone ought to dig), but why me?" However, there is hope yet for the moralist. To the retort "Why me?" the argument may not suggest any obvious reply; but the retort itself does suggest the counterretort "Why not you?", to which again there is no obvious reply. An impasse is thus reached in which the moralist cannot say why the defaulter should vote or dig, and the defaulter cannot say why he should not. Evidently it was a mistake to amend the original argument, and yet there seemed to be something wrong with it as it stood; and yet, as it stood, it still seemed to be giving an answer, however obscurely, to the baffling question "Why me?": "Because if *everyone* did that . . ."

To return to the camp: certainly it is agreed by all members of the party that some digging ought to be done, and it is also agreed that the duty does not lie on anyone outside the party. But just where it lies within the party is hard to say. It does not lie on everyone, nor on anyone in particular. Where then? Whatever the answer to that apparently pressing question may be, we all know what would in fact happen. Someone would volunteer, or a leader would allot duties, or the whole party would cast lots. Or, if the thing to be done were not a once-and-for-all job like digging latrines but a daily routine like washing up, they might take it in turns.

Although various acceptable answers to the question how the duties are to be allotted are readily listed, they leave us quite in the dark as to just *who* ought to dig, wash up, and so forth. That question hardly seems to arise. In the absence of an argumentative defaulter there is no call to think up reasons why I or you should do this or that or reasons why I or you should not, and we are left with the defaulter's "Why me?" and the moralist's "Why not you?" unanswered.

Our enquiry has made little progress, but the fog is beginning to lift from the territory ahead. We are evidently concerned with communities of people and with things that must be done, or not done, if the community is to be saved from damage or destruction; and we want to know whose duty it is to do, or not to do, these things. The complexity of the problem is no longer in doubt. (1) There are some things that need doing once, some that need doing at regular intervals, and some that need doing all the time. (2) Some things need doing by one person, some by a number of people which can be roughly estimated, and some by as many as possible. (3) In practice, who shall do what (though not who *ought* to do what) is determined by economic factors, or by statutory direction (*e.g.* service with the armed forces in war, paying income tax), or merely by people's inclinations generally, that is, when enough people are inclined to do the thing anyway.

Somewhere in this territory our quarry has its lair. The following dialogue between defaulter and moralist on the evasion of income tax and military service begins the hunt. Our first steps are taken on already familiar ground:

Defaulter. £100 is a drop in the ocean to the exchequer. No one will suffer from their loss of £100, but it means a good deal to me.

Moralist. But what if everyone did that and offered the same excuse?

D. But the vast majority won't, so no one will suffer.

M. Still, would you say it was *in order* for anyone whatever to evade tax and excuse himself on the same grounds as you do?

D. Certainly.

M. So it would be quite in order for *everyone* to do the same and offer the same excuse?

D. Yes.

M. Even though disaster would ensue for the exchequer and for everyone?

D. Yes. The exchequer would no more miss my £100 if *everyone* evaded than they would if only I evaded. They wouldn't miss anyone's individual evasion. What they would miss would be the aggregate £1,000,000,000 or so, and that isn't my default or yours or anyone's. So even if everyone evades it is still all right for me to evade; and if it's all right for me to evade it's all right for everyone to evade.

M. You seem now to be in the paradoxical position of saying that if everyone evaded it would be disastrous, and yet no one would be to blame.

D. Paradoxical, perhaps, but instructive. I am not alarmed. Let me recur to one of your previous questions: you asked whether it would be in order for all to evade and give the same excuse. I now want to reply: No, it would not be in order, but only in the sense that it would be disastrous; but it *would* be in order in the sense that each person's grounds for evasion would still be as valid as they would have been if he had been the *only* evader and no disaster had ensued. In other words, none of the defaulters would be to blame for the disaster—and certainly not one of them would blame himself: on the contrary, each one would argue that had he paid he would have been the only one to pay and thus lost his £100 without doing himself or anyone else any good. He would have been a mug to pay.

M. But surely there can't be a disaster of this kind for which no one is to blame.

D. If anyone is to blame it is the person whose job it is to circumvent evasion. If too few people vote, then it should be made illegal not to vote. If too few people volunteer, then you must introduce conscription. If too many people evade taxes, then you must tighten up your system of enforcement. My answer to your "If everyone did that" is: Then someone had jolly well better see to it that they don't; it doesn't impress me as a reason why *I* should, however many people do or don't.

M. But surely you are being inconsistent here. Take the case of evading military service.

D. You mean not volunteering in time of crisis, there being no conscription? I do that too.

M. Good. As I was saying, aren't you being inconsistent? You think *both* that it is all right not to volunteer even if too few other people volunteer (because one soldier more or less could make no difference), *and* think that you ought to be conscripted.

D. But that is not at all inconsistent. Look: the enemy threatens, a mere handful volunteer, and the writing is on the wall; my volunteering will not affect the outcome, but conscript me with the rest to stay the deluge and I will come without a murmur. In short, no good will come of my volunteering, but a great good will come of a general conscription which gathers me in with the rest. There is no inconsistency. I should add that my volunteering would in fact do positive harm: all who resist and survive are to be executed forthwith. There will be one or two heroes, but I did not think you were requiring me to be heroic.

M. I confirm that I was not, and I concede that your opinion is not inconsistent, however unedifying. As I see it, the nub of your position is this: Given the premiss "if everyone did that the result would be disastrous" you cannot conclude "therefore *you* oughtn't" but only "therefore someone ought to see to it that they don't." If you are right, the "if everyone did" argument, as usually taken, is invalid. But then we are left with the question: Whence does it derive its apparent force?

D. Whence, indeed?

(interval)

M. Suppose when you give your justification for evading ("no one will miss *my* contribution") I reply: But don't you think it *unfair* that other people should bear the burden which you shirk and from the bearing of which by others you derive benefit for yourself?

D. Well, yes, it is rather unfair. Indeed you make me feel a little ashamed; but I wasn't prepared, and I'm still not, to let your pet argument by without a fight. Just where does fairness come into it?

M. I think I can see. Let me begin by pushing two or three counters from different points on the periphery of the problem with the hope that they will meet at the centre. First, then: if someone is morally obliged (or permitted or forbidden) to do some particular thing, then there is a reason why he is so obliged. Further, if someone is obliged to do something for a particular reason, then anyone else whatever is equally obliged provided the reason applies to him also. The reason why a particular person is obliged to do something will be expressible in general terms, and could be expressed by describing some class to which he belongs. My principle then reads as follows: If someone is obliged to do something *just because* he is a member of a certain class, then any other member of that class will be equally obliged to do that thing. You yourself argued, remember, that any member of the class of people whose contribution would not be missed (here I allude to your reason for evasion) was no less entitled to evade than you.

D. Agreed.

M. My second counter now comes into play. "Fairness," you will agree, is a moral term like "rightness." An act is unfair if it results in someone getting a greater or lesser share of something (whether pleasant or unpleasant) than he ought to get—more or less than his fair share, as we say.

Now there are a number of things, burdensome or otherwise, which need to be done if the community is not to suffer. But who precisely is to do them? Why me? Why not me? You will also agree, I hope, to the wide principle that where the thing to be done is burdensome the burden should be fairly distributed?

D. Certainly. I seldom dispute a truism. But in what does a fair distribution consist?

M. In other words: given two people and a burden, how much of it ought each to bear? I say: *unless there is some reason why one should bear more or less of it than the other, they should both bear the same amount.* This is my Fairness Principle. It concerns both the fair allocation of the burden to some class of community members and the fair distribution of it within that class (and this may mean dividing the class into sub-classes of "isophoric" members): there must always be a *reason* for treating people differently. For instance, people who are unfit or above or below a certain age are exempted or excluded from military service, and for good reasons; women are exempted or excluded from certain kinds of military service, for what Plato regarded as bad reasons; those with more income pay more tax, while those with more children pay less, and for good reasons—and so on. You will have noticed that the typical complaint about unfair dealing begins with a "why": "Why did they charge me more than him?" (unfair distribution), or "Why should married couples be liable for so much surtax?" (unfair allocation). The maxim governing differential treatment, that is, which is behind the reasons given for it, seems to be: From each according to his resources, to each according to his need. You might argue that my principle about equal burdens is no more than a special case of this maxim. But that principle is all I need for my argument and all I insist on; I shall not stick my neck out further than necessary.

D. It is not, thus far, too dangerously exposed, I think.

M. Good. We are now ready to move a little nearer to the core of the problem. But first compare the two principles I have advanced. The first was: if a thing is obligatory and so forth for one person, then it is obligatory and so forth for anyone in the same class (*i.e.* the class relevant to the reason given). This is a license to argue from one member of a class to all its members; we will call it the Universalization Principle (U-Principle). The second, which is my Fairness Principle, is: A burden laid on a particular class is to be shared equally by all its members, unless there is reason to the contrary. This, in contrast to the first, is a license to argue from the class itself to each of its members. I take it, by the way, that these two principles are independent, that neither follows from the other.

D. Granted, granted. I am impatient to know what light all this throws on your "if everyone did" argument.

M. I am coming to that. You will remember that you used the U-Principle yourself to argue that if it's all right for you to evade it's all right for everyone else. But it was no use to me in pressing my case, and we can now see why: it argues from one to all, and there was no *one* to argue from. Nor, of course, could I argue from the consequences of your act. "Why me?" you asked, and I had then no reply. But I did at least have a retort: "Why not you?" Now it seems to me that it is just my Fairness Principle that lies behind the effectiveness of this retort, for by it you can be shown to have a duty in cases like this unless you can show that you have not. You would have to show, in the military service example, that you were not a member of the class on which the duty of military service is normally (and we will assume, fairly) regarded as lying. But you cannot show this: you cannot claim to be under age or over age or blind or lame. All you claim is that you have a certain property, the property of being one whose contribution won't be missed, which is shared by every other member of the military class; and this claim, so far from being a good reason for not volunteering, now stands revealed as no reason at all.

D. Still, you didn't dispute my point that the blame for a disaster following upon wholesale evasion lay upon those duty it was, or in whose power it lay, to prevent such evasion.

M. You certainly had a point, but I can see now that you made too much of it. I concede that the authorities failed in their duty, but then the military class as a whole failed in theirs too. The duty of both was ultimately the same, to ensure the safety of the state, just as the duty of wicket-keeper and long-stop is the same, to save byes. To confine the blame to the authorities is like saying that it's all right to burn the house down so long as it's insured or that the mere existence of a police force constitutes a general license to rob banks. As for the individual defaulter, you wanted to absolve him from all blame— a claim which seemed at once plausible and paradoxical: plausible because he was not, as you rightly pointed out, to blame for the disaster (it was not his duty to prevent that, since it was not in his power to do so); paradoxical because he was surely to blame for *something*, and we now know what for: failure to bear his share of the burden allotted to his class.

D. Maybe, but it still seems to me that if I volunteer and others don't I shall be taking on an unfair share of it, and *that* can't be fair. Then again if I don't volunteer I shall be doing less than my share, and *that* can't be fair either. Whichever I do, there's something wrong. And that can't be right.

M. There are two mistakes here. Whichever you do there's something wrong, but nothing unfair; the only wrong is people failing in their duty. Fairness is an attribute of distributions, and whether you volunteer or not neither you nor anyone else are distributing anything. Nor, for that matter, are fate or circumstances, for they are not persons. That is your first mistake. Your second is this: you talk as if the lone volunteer will necessarily do more than his fair share. He may, but he needn't. If he does, that is his own look out: *volenti non fit iniuria*.

D. It's more dangerous to fight alone than as one among many. How can he ration the danger?

M. He can surrender or run away. Look, he isn't expected to be heroic or to do, or even attempt, the impossible. If two are needed to launch and man the lifeboat, the lone volunteer can only stand and wait: *he also* serves. The least a man can do is offer and hold himself ready, though sometimes it is also the most he can do.

D. Let it be so. But I am still in trouble about one thing: suppose I grant all you say about fairness and the defaulter, I'm still not clear why you choose to make your point against him in just the mysterious way you do, that is, by fixing him with your glittering eye and beginning "If everyone did that."

M. It is a little puzzling, isn't it? But not all that puzzling. After all, the premiss states and implies a good deal: (1) It states that wholesale evasion will have such and such results; (2) it states or implies that the results will be bad; (3) it implies strongly that a duty to prevent them must lie *somewhere*; (4) it implies that the duty does not lie solely on the person addressed (otherwise a quite different kind of argument would apply); (5) it implies, rather weakly, that nevertheless the person addressed has no better excuse for doing nothing about it than anyone else has. The conclusion is then stated that he ought to do something about it. A gap remains, to be sure; but it can't be a very big one, or people wouldn't, as they sometimes do, feel the force of the argument, however obscurely. The "Why me?" retort brings out implication (4), while the "Why not you?" counterretort brings out implication (5); and we didn't really have very far to go from there.

The argument is clearly elliptical and needs filling out with some explicit reference to the Fairness Principle. I would formulate it as follows:

> Unless such and such is done, undesirable consequences X will ensue;
>
> the burden of preventing X lies upon class Y as a whole;
>
> each member of class Y has a *prima facie* duty to bear an equal share of the burden by doing Z;
>
> you are a member of class Y;
>
> therefore you have a *prima facie* duty to do Z.

I have introduced the notion of a *prima facie* duty at this late stage to cover those cases where only a few members of class Y are required to do Z and it would be silly to put them all to work. In the latrine case only one person needs to dig, and in America only a small proportion of fit persons are required for short-term military service. In such cases it is considered fair to select the requisite number by lot. Until the lot is cast I must hold myself ready; if I am selected my *prima facie* duty becomes an actual duty; if I am spared, it lapses. Why selection by lot should be a fair method I leave you to work out for yourself.

Notice that the argument only holds if the thing to be done is burdensome. Voting isn't really very burdensome; indeed a lot of people seem to enjoy it, and this accounts for the weakness of the argument in this application. If the thing to be done were positively enjoyable one might even have to invoke the Fairness Principle against overindulgence.

Notice, finally, that the argument doesn't apply unless there is a fairly readily isolable class to which a burden can be allotted. This rules out the farming and such like cases. You can't lay it down that the burden of providing food for the nation (if it *is* a burden) lies on the farmers (*i.e.* the class that provides food for the nation), for that is a tautology, or perhaps it implies the curious proposition that everyone *ought* to be doing the job he *is* doing. Might one say instead that *everyone* has a *prima facie* duty to farm, but that the duty lapses when inclination, ability and economic reward conspire to select a sufficient farming force? Far-fetched, I think. The matter might be pursued, but only at the risk of tedium. Well, are you satisfied?

D. Up to a point. Your hypothesis obviously calls for a lot more testing yet. But I have carried the burden a good deal further than my fair share of the distance; let others take it from here.

A Critique of Kantianism

RICHARD TAYLOR

Richard Taylor (b. 1919) is a professor of philosophy at the University of Rochester. He writes in the areas of ethics and metaphysics. Among his many books are *Good and Evil* and *With Heart and Mind*. He is also an expert on bees.

Taylor criticizes Kant's moral philosophy for being too abstract and intellectual. We ordinarily think of a person of goodwill as someone with a kindly and sympathetic nature. Not so for Kant. His person of goodwill acts from respect for the moral law. To Kant, acts done solely out of kindness and sympathy have no moral worth. Taylor recommends a moral system less abstract and metaphysical and more compatible with human nature.

A CRITIQUE OF KANTIANISM   Reprinted from *Good and Evil* by Richard Taylor, © 1984 by Richard Taylor, by permission of Prometheus Books, 700 East Amherst St., Buffalo, NY 14215.

Taylor's rejection of Kant's impersonal approach should be compared with Richard Peters's more sympathetic attempt to derive a humanized form of Kantianism.

It is not my intention to give any detailed exposition of Kant's ethical system. I propose instead to discuss certain of Kant's basic ideas in order to illustrate a certain approach to ethics that I think is essentially wrong. For this I could have chosen the ideas of some other modern moralist, but I prefer to illustrate my points by Kant's thought. I am doing this first because of his great fame and the reverence with which many philosophers still regard him, and secondly because it would be difficult to find any modern thinker who has carried to such an extreme the philosophical presuppositions that I am eager to repudiate. I shall, thus, use some of Kant's ideas to show how the basic ideas of morality, born originally of men's practical needs as social beings and having to do originally with men's practical relations with each other, can, under the influence of philosophy, become so detached from the world that they become pure abstractions, having no longer anything to do with morality insofar as this is a practical concern of men. Philosophical or metaphysical morals thereby ceases to have much connection with the morality that is the abiding practical concern of men and becomes, instead, a purely intellectual thing, something to contemplate and appreciate, much as one would appreciate a geometrical demonstration. Its vocabulary, which is the very vocabulary of everyday morals, no longer has the same meaning, but instead represents a realm of pure abstractions. Intellectually satisfying as this might be, it is nevertheless highly dangerous, for it leads men to suppose that the problems of ethics are essentially intellectual problems, that they are simply philosophical questions in need of philosophical answers. The result is that the eyes of the moralist are directed away from the world, in which moral problems are the most important problems there are, and toward a really nonexistent realm, a realm of ideas rather than things. The image of the philosophical and metaphysical moralist, who is quite lacking in any knowledge of the world and whose ideas about it are of the childish sort learned in a Sunday school, is a familiar one. He is a moralist whose dialectic is penetrating and whose reasoning is clear—he grapples with many philosophical problems of morality and has many subtle answers to philosophical difficulties—but who has little appreciation of the pain and sorrow of the world beyond the knowledge that it is there.

Duty and Law

Laws, as practical rules of human invention, find no place in Kant's metaphysical morals. The Moral Law that replaces them is sundered from any practical human concerns, for it seemed to Kant that men's practical ends and their moral obligations were not only quite different things but, more often than not, were actually opposed to each other. Obligations, which were originally only relations between men arising from mutual undertakings for mutual advantage, similarly disappear from the Kantian morality, to be replaced by an abstract sort of *moral* obligation that has no connection whatsoever with any earthly good. Duties—which were originally and are still imposed by rulers on subjects, masters on servants, employers on workmen, and so on, in return for certain compensations, privileges, and rights—are replaced by Kant with Duty in the abstract. This abstract Duty is deemed by him to be the sole proper motive of moral conduct; yet, it is not a duty *to* anyone, or a duty to do any particular thing. Men have always understood the notion of one's duty to sovereign or master, and Christians well understood the idea of duty toward God. In such cases, one's duty consisted simply of compliance with commands. But in Kant's system, duties are sundered from particular commands, and Duty becomes something singular and metaphysical. We are, according to this system, to do always what Duty requires, for no other reason than that Duty does require it. Beyond a few heterogeneous examples for illustration, we never learn from Kant just what this is, save only that it is the obligation to act from respect for the Moral Law. A man must cling to life, for example, and give no thought to suicide—not because any lawgiver or God has commanded it, not because things might work out all right for him if he sticks it out a little longer, but just because Duty requires it. A man must also help others in distress; not, again, because any man or God has admonished him to, not just because they need him, or because he cares for them, or because he wants to see their baneful condition improved—indeed, it is best that he have no such feelings at all—but just because it is his Duty.

The Good Will

It is in such terms that Kant defined the *good will*, declaring it to be the only thing in the universe that is unqualifiedly good. Now we normally think of a man of good will as one who loves his fellow men, as one whose happiness is sympathetically bound up with that of others, and as one who has a keen and constant desire to abolish the suffering around him and make the lot of his neighbor more tolerable than it might be without his helping hand. Not so for Kant. Indeed, he dismisses the actions of such persons, "so sympathetically constituted that . . . they find an inner satisfaction in spreading joy, and rejoice in the contentment of others which they have made possible," as devoid of any moral worth. Human conduct, to have any genuine moral worth, must not spring from any such amiable feelings as these; these are, after all, nothing but human feelings; they are not *moral* incentives. To have genuine moral worth, according to this moralist, our actions must spring from the sense of Duty and nothing else. And one acts dutifully if he acts, not from love or concern for his fellows, but from respect for the Moral Law.

The Categorical Imperative

The Moral Law assumed, in Kant's thought, the form of an imperative, or command. But unlike any command that was ever before heard by any man, this one issues from no commander! Like a question that no one ever asks, or an assertion that no one ever affirms, it is a command that no God or man ever promulgates. It is promulgated by Reason. Nor is this the humble rationality of living, mortal men; it is Reason itself, again in the abstract. And unlike what one would ordinarily think of as a command, this one has no definite content. It is simply the form, Kant says, not of any actual laws, but of The Law, which is again, of course, something abstract. It has, unlike any other imperative of which one has ever heard, no purpose or end. It is not the means to the achievement of anything; and it has no relation to what anyone wants. For this reason Kant called it the Categorical Imperative, a command that is supposed to command absolutely and for its own sake. The Categorical Imperative does not bid us to act in a manner calculated to advance human well-being, for the weal and woe of men has for Kant no necessary connection with morality. It does not bid us to act as we would want others to act, for what any men want has no more bearing on morals than what they happen to feel. This Imperative does not, in fact, bid us to do anything at all, nor, indeed, even to have any generous or sympathetic motive, but only to honor some maxim or rational principle of conduct. We are, whatever we do, to act in such a manner that we could, consistently with reason, will this maxim to be a universal Law, even a Law of Nature, binding on all rational beings. Kant does not ask us to consider how other rational beings, thus bound, might feel about our maxims, for again, how anyone happens to feel about anything has no bearing on morality anyway. It is Reason that counts. It is not the living and suffering human beings who manage sometimes to be reasonable but most of the time are not. It is not men's needs and wants, or any human desires, or any practical human goods. To act immorally is to act contrary to Reason; it is to commit a sort of metaphysical blunder in the relationship between one's behavior and his generalized motive. Human needs and feelings have so little to do with this that they are not even allowed into the picture. If a man reaches forth to help the sick, the troubled, or the dying, this must not be done from any motive of compassion or sentiment of love. Such love, as a feeling, is dismissed by Kant as "pathological," because it is not prompted by that rational respect for Duty that filled Kant with such awe. Indeed, Kant thought that such human feelings as love and compassion should not even be allowed to cooperate in the performance of Duty, for we must act solely *from* Duty, and not merely *in accordance* with it. Such feelings as love, sympathy, and friendship are therefore regarded by Kant as positively dangerous. They incline men to do from sheer goodness of heart what should be done only from Reason and respect for the Moral Law. To be genuinely moral, a man must tear himself away from his inclinations as a loving human being, drown the sympathetic promptings of his heart, scorn any fruits of his efforts, think last of all of the feelings, needs, desires, and inclinations either of himself or of his fellows and, perhaps detesting what he has to do, do it anyway—solely from respect for the Law.

Rational Nature as an End

This Moral Law is otherwise represented by Kant as respect for Rational Nature, something that again, of course, exists only in the abstract but is, presumably, somehow exemplified in men and, Kant thought, in God. Indeed, it is the only thing in men that Kant considered worthy of a philosopher's attention. Because men are deemed to embody this Rational Nature, human nature is declared to be an End in Itself, to possess an absolute Worth, or Dignity. This kind of absolute End is not like ordinary ends or goals, something relative to the aims or purposes of any creature. It is not anything anyone wants or would be moved to try to achieve. It is, like so many of Kant's abstractions, an absolute end. And the Worth that he supposes Rational Nature to possess is no worth *for* or *to* anything; it, too, is an abstract or absolute Worth. Kant peoples a veritable utopia, which he of course does not imagine as existing, with these Ends in Themselves, and calls it the Kingdom of Ends. Ends in Themselves are, thus, not to be thought of as those men that live and toil on earth; they are not suffering, rejoicing, fumbling, living, and dying human beings; they are not men that anyone has ever seen, or would be apt to recognize as men if he did see them, or apt to like very much if he did recognize them. They are abstract things, reifications of Rational Nature, fabricated by Kant and now called Rational Beings or Ends in Themselves. Their purpose, unlike that of any creature under the sun, is not to sorrow and rejoice, not to love and hate, not to beget offspring, not to grow old and die, and not to get on as best they can to such destinies as the world has allotted them. Their purpose is just to *legislate*—to legislate morally and rationally for this rational Kingdom of Ends.

The Significance of Kant

Kant's system thus represents the rational, logical conclusion of the natural or true morality that was begotten by the Greeks, of the absolute distinction that they drew, and that men still want to draw. This is the distinction between what *is*, or the realm of observation and science, and what *ought* to be, or the realm of obligation and morals. No one has ever suggested that Kant was irrational, and although it is doubtful that his ideas have ever had much impact on human behavior, they have had a profound impact on philosophy, which has always prized reason and abstraction and tended to scorn fact. Kant's metaphysical system of morals rests on notions that are still a part of the fabric of our intellectual culture and inheritance. His greatest merit is that he was consistent. He showed men what sort of metaphysic of morals they must have—if they suppose that morality has any metaphysic, or any logic and method of its own. He showed what morality must be if we suppose it to be something rational and at the same time nonempirical or divorced from psychology, anthropology, or any science of man. That general conception of morals is, of course, still common in philosophy, and still permeates judicial thought, where it expresses itself in the ideas of guilt and desert. A man is thought to be "deserving" of punishment if he did, and could have avoided doing, something "wrong." Our basic moral presuppositions, in short, are still very much the same as Kant's, and Kant shows where they lead. We still assume, as he did, a basic dichotomy between what in fact *is* and what morally *ought* to be, between what the Greeks called convention and nature. Like the Greeks, and like Kant, we still feel a desperate need to *know* what, by nature or by some natural or rational moral principle, *ought* to be. Kant was entirely right in insisting that no knowledge of what in fact is—no knowledge of human nature, of history, of anthropology, or psychology—can yield this knowledge. But Kant did not consider, and many philosophical minds still think it somehow perverse to consider, that there may be no such knowledge—and not merely because no man has managed to attain it, but because there may really be nothing there to know in the first place. There may be no such thing as a true morality. Perhaps the basic facts of morality are, as Protagoras thought, conventions; that is, the practical formulas, some workable and some not, for enabling men to achieve whatever ideals and aspirations happen to move them. In the Kantian scheme, such considerations have nothing to do with morality which is concerned, not with what is, but with what morally ought to be, with what is in his strange sense commanded. According to the Protagorean scheme, on the other hand, such considerations exhaust the whole subject of morals. Here we are, human beings, possessed of needs, feelings, capacities, and aims that are for the most part not of our creation but are simply part of our endowment as human beings. These are the grist, the data, and the subject matter of morals. The problem is how we get from where we are to where we want to go. It is on our answer to this question that our whole happiness and our worth as human beings depends. Our problem is not whether our answers accord with nature or even with truth. Our problem is to find those answers that do in fact work, whose fruits are sunlight, warmth, and satisfaction in our lives as we live them.

Chapter

2

UTILITARIANISM

The Principle of Utility

JEREMY BENTHAM

Jeremy Bentham (1748–1832) is the father of modern Utilitarianism. He was one of the leading political philosophers of his time, and his book *The Principles of Morals and Legislation* is a classic of moral and political philosophy.

According to Bentham's "principle of utility," actions are right when they increase happiness and diminish misery, wrong when they have the opposite effect. By "utility" he means the property of producing pleasure or happiness in conscious beings. Thus we should always do those acts that tend to increase overall happiness. Bentham is known as a "hedonistic utilitarian": pleasure is to be pursued, pain to be avoided. A legislator, for example, should calculate the pleasure/pain ratio of each prospective law. Bentham proposes that we evaluate pleasures according to their intensity, duration, certainty, propinquity (nearness), fecundity (tendency to lead to other pleasures), purity (tendency *not* to be followed by pain), and, finally, extent (the number of persons to whom the pleasure extends). Bentham concedes that he cannot *prove* the truth of the principle of utility; but he claims that most of us implicitly accept it and act on it every day. And he suspects that any alternative principle will be "despotical, and hostile to all the rest of the human race."

THE PRINCIPLE OF UTILITY   Excerpted from Jeremy Bentham, *The Principles of Morals and Legislation* (1789).

The principle of utility is the foundation of the present work: it will be proper therefore at the outset to give an explicit and determinate account of what is meant by it. By the principle of utility is meant that principle which approves or disapproves of every action whatsoever, according to the tendency which it appears to have to augment or diminish the happiness of the party whose interest is in question: or, what is the same thing in other words, to promote or to oppose that happiness. I say of every action whatsoever; and therefore not only of every action of a private individual, but of every measure of government.

By utility is meant that property in any object, whereby it tends to produce benefit, advantage, pleasure, good, or happiness (all this in the present case comes to the same thing), or (what comes again to the same thing) to prevent the happening of mischief, pain, evil, or unhappiness to the party whose interest is considered: if that party be the community in general, then the happiness of the community: if a particular individual, then the happiness of that individual.

The interest of the community is one of the most general expressions that can occur in the phraseology of morals: no wonder that the meaning of it is often lost. When it has a meaning, it is this. The community is a fictitious *body*, composed of the individual persons who are considered as constituting as it were its *members*. The interest of the community then is, what?—the sum of the interests of the several members who compose it.

It is in vain to talk of the interests of the community, without understanding what is the interest of the individual. A thing is said to promote the interest, or to be *for* the interest, of an individual, when it tends to add to the sum total of his pleasures: or, what comes to the same thing, to diminish the sum total of his pains.

An action then may be said to be conformable to the principle of utility, or, for shortness sake, to utility (meaning with respect to the community at large), when the tendency it has to augment the happiness of the community is greater than any it has to diminish it.

A measure of government (which is but a particular kind of action, performed by a particular person or persons) may be said to be conformable to or dictated by the principle of utility, when in like manner the tendency which it has to augment the happiness of the community is greater than any which it has to diminish it.

When an action, or in particular a measure of government, is supposed by a man to be conformable to the principle of utility, it may be convenient, for the purposes of discourse, to imagine a kind of law or dictate, called a law or dictate of utility: and to speak of the action in question, as being conformable to such law or dictate.

A man may be said to be a partizan of the principle of utility, when the approbation or disapprobation he annexes to any action, or to any measure, is determined by and proportioned to the tendency which he conceives it to have to augment or to diminish the happiness of the community: or in other words, to its conformity or unconformity to the laws or dictates of utility.

Of an action that is conformable to the principle of utility one may always say either that it is one that ought to be done, or at least that it is not one that ought not to be done. One may say also, that it is right it should be done; at least that it is not wrong it should be done: that it is a right action; at least that it is not a wrong action. When thus interpreted, the words *ought*, and *right* and *wrong*, and others of that stamp, have a meaning: when otherwise, they have none.

Has the rectitude of this principle been ever formally contested? It should seem that it had, by those who have not known what they have been meaning. Is it susceptible of any direct proof? it should seem not: for that which is used to prove every thing else, cannot itself be proved: a chain of proofs must have their commencement somewhere. To give such proof is as impossible as it is needless.

Not that there is or ever has been that human creature breathing, however stupid or perverse, who has not on many, perhaps on most occasions of his life, deferred to it. By the natural constitution of the human frame, on most occasions of their lives men in general embrace this principle, without thinking of it: if not for the ordering of their own actions, yet for the trying of their own actions, as well as of those of other men. There have been, at the same time, not many, perhaps, even of the most intelligent, who have been disposed to embrace it purely and without reserve. There are even few who have not taken some occasion or other to quarrel with it, either on account of their not understanding always how to apply it, or on account of some prejudice or other which they were afraid to examine into, or could not bear to part with. For such is the stuff that man is made of: in principle and in practice, in a right track and in a wrong one, the rarest of all human qualities is consistency.

When a man attempts to combat the principle of utility, it is with reasons drawn, without his being aware of it, from that very principle itself. His arguments, if they prove any thing, prove not that the principle is *wrong*, but that, according to the applications he supposes to be made of it, it is *misapplied*. Is it possible for a man to move the earth? Yes; but he must first find out another earth to stand upon.

To disprove the propriety of it by arguments is impossible; but, from the causes that have been mentioned, or from some confused or partial view of it, a man may happen to be disposed not to relish it. Where this is the case, if he thinks the settling of his opinions on such a subject worth the trouble, let him take the following steps, and at length, perhaps, he may come to reconcile himself to it.

Let him settle with himself, whether he would wish to discard this principle altogether; if so, let him consider what it is that all his reasonings (in matters of politics especially) can amount to?

If he would, let him settle with himself, whether he would judge and act without any principle, or whether there is any other he would judge and act by?

If there be, let him examine and satisfy himself whether the principle he thinks he has found is really any separate intelligible principle; or whether it be not a mere principle in words, a kind of phrase, which at bottom expresses neither more nor less than the mere averment of his own unfounded sentiments; that is, what in another person he might be apt to call caprice?

If he is inclined to think that his own approbation or disapprobation, annexed to the idea of an act, without any regard to its consequences, is a sufficient foundation for him to judge and act upon, let him ask himself whether his sentiment is to be a standard of right and wrong, with respect to every other man, or whether every man's sentiment has the same privilege of being a standard to itself?

In the first case, let him ask himself whether his principle is not despotical, and hostile to all the rest of human race?

In the second case, whether it is not anarchial, and whether at this rate there are not as many different standards of right and wrong as there are men? and whether even to the same man, the same thing, which is right to-day, may not (without the least change in its nature) be wrong to-morrow? and whether the same thing is not right and wrong in the same place at the same time? and in either

75

CHAPTER TWO/UTILITARIANISM

case, whether all argument is not at an end? and whether, when two men have said, "I like this," and "I don't like it," they can (upon such a principle) have any thing more to say?

If he should have said to himself, No: for that the sentiment which he proposes as a standard must be grounded on reflection, let him say on what particulars the reflection is to turn? if on particulars having relation to the utility of the act, then let him say whether this is not deserting his own principle and borrowing assistance from that very one in opposition to which he sets it up: or if not on those particulars, on what other particulars?

If he should be for compounding the matter, and adopting his own principle in part, and the principle of utility in part, let him say how far he will adopt it?

When he has settled with himself where he will stop, then let him ask himself how he justifies to himself the adopting it so far? and why he will not adopt it any farther?

Admitting any other principle than the principle of utility to be a right principle, a principle that it is right for a man to pursue; admitting (what is not true) that the word *right* can have a meaning without reference to utility, let him say whether there is any such thing as a *motive* that a man can have to pursue the dictates of it: if there is, let him say what that motive is, and how it is to be distinguished from those which enforce the dictates of utility: if not, then lastly let him say what it is this other principle can be good for?

Pleasures then, and the avoidance of pains, are the *ends* which the legislator has in view: it behoves him therefore to understand their *value*. Pleasures and pains are the *instruments* he has to work with: it behoves him therefore to understand their force, which is again, in other words, their value.

To a person considered *by himself*, the value of a pleasure or pain considered *by itself*, will be greater or less, according to the four following circumstances:

1. Its *intensity*.
2. Its *duration*.
3. Its *certainty* or *uncertainty*.
4. Its *propinquity* or *remoteness*.

These are the circumstances which are to be considered in estimating a pleasure or a pain considered each of them by itself. But when the value of any pleasure or pain is considered for the purpose of estimating the tendency of any *act* by which it is produced, there are two other circumstances to be taken into the account; these are,

5. Its *fecundity*, or the chance it has of being followed by sensations of the *same* kind: that is, pleasures, if it be a pleasure: pains, if it be a pain.

6. Its *purity*, or the chance it has of *not* being followed by sensations of the *opposite* kind: that is, pains, if it be a pleasure: pleasures, if it be a pain.

These two last, however, are in strictness scarcely to be deemed properties of the pleasure or the pain itself; they are not, therefore, in strictness to be taken into the account of the value of that pleasure or that pain. They are in strictness to be deemed properties only of the act, or other event, by which such pleasure or pain has been produced; and accordingly are only to be taken into the account of the tendency of such act or such event.

To a *number* of persons, with reference to each of whom the value of a pleasure or a pain is considered, it will be greater or less, according to seven circumstances: to wit, the six preceding ones; *viz.*

1. Its *intensity.*
2. Its *duration.*
3. Its *certainty* or *uncertainty.*
4. Its *propinquity* or *remoteness.*
5. Its *fecundity.*
6. Its *purity.*

And one other; to wit:

7. Its *extent*; that is, the number of persons to whom it *extends*; or (in other words) who are affected by it.

To take an exact account then of the general tendency of any act, by which the interests of a community are affected, proceed as follows. Begin with any one person of those whose interests seem most immediately to be affected by it: and take an account,

1. Of the value of each distinguishable *pleasure* which appears to be produced by it in the *first* instance.

2. Of the value of each *pain* which appears to be produced by it in the *first* instance.

3. Of the value of each pleasure which appears to be produced by it *after* the first. This constitutes the *fecundity* of the first *pleasure* and the *inpurity* of the first *pain.*

4. Of the value of each *pain* which appears to be produced by it after the first. This constitutes the *fecundity* of the first *pain*, and the *impurity* of the first pleasure.

5. Sum up all the values of all the *pleasures* on the one side, and those of all the pains on the other. The balance, if it be on the side of pleasure, will give the *good* tendency of the act upon the whole, with respect to the interests of that *individual* person; if on the side of pain, the *bad* tendency of it upon the whole.

6. Take an account of the *number* of persons whose interests appear to be concerned; and repeat the above process with respect to each. *Sum* up the numbers expressive of the degrees of *good* tendency, which the act has, with respect to each individual, in regard to whom the tendency of it is *good* upon the whole: do this again with respect to each individual, in regard to whom the tendency of it is *good* upon the whole: do this again with respect to each individual, in regard to whom the tendency of it is *bad* upon the whole. Take the *balance*; which, if on the side of *pleasure*, will give the general *good tendency* of the act, with respect to the total number or community of individuals concerned; if on the side of pain, the general *evil tendency*, with respect to the same community.

It is not to be expected that this process should be strictly pursued previously to every moral judgment, or to every legislative or judicial operation. It may, however, be always kept in view: and as near as the process actually pursued on these occasions approaches to it, so near will such process approach to the character of an exact one.

The same process is alike applicable to pleasure and pain, in whatever shape they appear: and by whatever denomination they are distinguished: to pleasure, whether it be called *good* (which is properly the cause or instrument of pleasure) or *profit* (which is distant pleasure, or the cause or instrument of distant pleasure), or *convenience*, or *advantage, benefit, emolument, happiness,* and so forth; to pain, whether it be called *evil* (which corresponds to *good*), or *mischief,* or *inconvenience*, or *disadvantage*, or *loss*, or *unhappiness*, and so forth.

Nor is this a novel and unwarranted, any more than it is a useless theory. In all this there is nothing but what the practice of mankind, whatsoever they have a clear view of their own interest, is perfectly conformable to. An article of property, an estate in land, for instance, is valuable, on what account? On account of the pleasures of all kinds which it enables a man to produce, and what comes to the same thing the pains of all kinds which it enables him to avert. But the value of such an article of property is universally understood to rise or fall according to the length or shortness of the time which a man has in it: the certainty or uncertainty of its coming into possession: and the nearness or remoteness of the time at which, if at all, it is to come into possession. As to the *intensity* of the pleasures which a man may derive from it, this is never thought of, because it depends upon the use which each particular person may come to make of it; which cannot be estimated till the particular pleasures he may come to derive from it, or the particular pains he may come to exclude by means of it, are brought to view. For the same reason, neither does he think of the *fecundity* or *purity* of those pleasures.

Utilitarianism

J. J. C. SMART

J. J. C. Smart (b. 1920) is a professor emeritus at the University of Adelaide and a professor of philosophy at the Australian National University. He is the author of several books, including *Philosophy and Scientific Realism* and *Ethics Persuasion and Truth*.

Act utilitarians tell us to choose *actions* that increase happiness and diminish misery. Rule utilitarianism, on the other hand, tells us to act according to *rules* that tend to increase happiness and diminish misery. Thus an act utilitarian might break a promise whenever the principle of utility favored doing so; according to rule utilitarianism, it is better all around if everyone follows the rules ("Keep

UTILITARIANISM   From "An Outline of a System of Utilitarian Ethics" in *Utilitarianism: For and Against*, edited by J. J. C. Smart and Bernard Williams. Reprinted by permission of Cambridge University Press.

your promises"; "Tell the truth") even when, in a particular case, adherence to the rule does not increase utility.
Smart is an act utilitarian, and he criticizes rule utilitarians for being "rule worshippers." Why, he asks, should
someone follow a rule in cases in which there is greater
utility in breaking it? Smart also considers the problem
of the "higher" and "lower" pleasures. It may well be
that a dog gets more pleasure chasing a rat than a philosopher does contemplating the mysteries of the universe.
Should we then try to reduce the number of discontented
philosophers and fill the world with happy dogs? Smart
answers that it is inaccurate to describe dogs as happy.
To call human beings happy, however, is not merely to
describe them as contented, but to express approval for
their form of contentness. Developing an idea of
Bentham, Smart argues that the higher pleasures of poetry, philosophy, and science tend to be more "fecund"
(that is, conducive to other pleasures) than the lower
pleasures, such as drunkeness, chasing rats, or playing
bingo. Smart addresses a number of other problems facing Utilitarianism: Should we try to increase the *average*
happiness of human beings or should we try to increase
the *total* amount of happiness in the world? Must we
consider the remote consequences of our actions? Is there
a place for rules in act utilitarianism? Smart believes that
act utilitarianism is a simple and natural doctrine that
will eventually appeal to all who care about the happiness
of humankind.

The system of normative ethics which I am here concerned to
defend is . . . *act*-utilitarianism. Act-utilitarianism is to be contrasted with rule-utilitarianism. Act-utilitarianism is the view that
the rightness or wrongness of an action is to be judged by the
consequences, good or bad, of the action itself. Rule-utilitarianism
is the view that the rightness or wrongness of an action is to be
judged by the goodness and badness of the consequences of a rule
that everyone should perform the action in like circumstances. . . .

I have argued elsewhere[1] the objections to rule-utilitarianism as compared with act-utilitarianism. Briefly they boil down to the accusation of rule worship: the rule-utilitarian presumably advocates his principle because he is ultimately concerned with human happiness: why then should he advocate abiding by a rule when he knows that it will not in the present case be most beneficial to abide by it? The reply that in most cases it is most beneficial to abide by the rule seems irrelevant. And so is the reply that it would be better that everybody should abide by the rule than that nobody should. This is to suppose that the only alternative to "everybody does A" is "no one does A." But clearly we have the possibility "some people do A and some don't." Hence to refuse to break a generally beneficial rule in those cases in which it is not most beneficial to obey it seems irrational and to be a case of rule worship.

The type of utilitarianism which I shall advocate will, then, be act-utilitarianism, not rule-utilitarianism. . . .

An act-utilitarian judges the rightness or wrongness of actions by the goodness and badness of their consequences. But is he to judge the goodness and badness of the consequences of an action solely by their pleasantness and unpleasantness? Bentham, who thought that quantity of pleasure being equal, the experience of playing pushpin was as good as that of reading poetry, could be classified as a hedonistic act-utilitarian. Moore, who believed that some states of mind, such as those of acquiring knowledge, had intrinsic value quite independent of their pleasantness, can be called an ideal utilitarian. Mill seemed to occupy an intermediate position. He held that there are higher and lower pleasures. This seems to imply that pleasure is a necessary condition for goodness but that goodness depends on other qualities of experience than pleasantness and unpleasantness. I propose to call Mill a quasi-ideal utilitarian. . . .

What Bentham, Mill and Moore are all agreed on is that the rightness of an action is to be judged solely by consequences, states of affairs brought about by the action. Of course we shall have to

---

[1]In my article "Extreme and restricted utilitarianism," *Philosophical Quarterly* 6 (1956) 344–54. This contains bad errors and a better version of the article will be found in Philippa Foot (ed.), *Theories of Ethics* (Oxford University Press, London, 1967), or Michael D. Bayles (ed.) *Contemporary Utilitarianism* (Doubleday, New York, 1968). In this article I used the terms "extreme" and "restricted" instead of Brandt's more felicitous "act" and "rule" which I now prefer.

be careful here not to construe "state of affairs" so widely that any ethical doctrine becomes utilitarian. For if we did so we would not be saying anything at all in advocating utilitarianism. If, for example, we allowed "the state of having just kept a promise," then a deontologist who said we should keep promises simply because they are promises would be a utilitarian. And we do not wish to allow this. . . . Let us consider Mill's contention that it is "better to be Socrates dissatisfied than a fool satisfied." Mill holds that pleasure is not to be our sole criterion for evaluating consequences: the state of mind of Socrates might be less pleasurable than that of the fool, but, according to Mill, Socrates would be happier than the fool.

It is necessary to observe, first of all, that a purely hedonistic utilitarian, like Bentham, might agree with Mill in preferring the experiences of discontented philosophers to those of contented fools. His preference for the philosopher's state of mind, however, would not be an *intrinsic* one. He would say that the discontented philosopher is a useful agent in society and that the existence of Socrates is responsible for an improvement in the lot of humanity generally. Consider two brothers. One may be of a docile and easy temperament: he may lead a supremely contented and unambitious life, enjoying himself hugely. The other brother may be ambitious, may stretch his talents to the full, may strive for scientific success and academic honours, and may discover some invention or some remedy for disease or improvement in agriculture which will enable innumerable men of easy temperament to lead a contented life, whereas otherwise they would have been thwarted by poverty, disease or hunger. Or he may make some advance in pure science which will later have beneficial practical applications. Or, again, he may write poetry which will solace the leisure hours and stimulate the brains of practical men or scientists, thus indirectly leading to an improvement in society. That is, the pleasures of poetry or mathematics may be *extrinsically* valuable in a way in which those of pushpin or sun-bathing may not be. Though the poet or mathematician may be discontented, society as a whole may be the more contented for his presence. . . .

Maybe we have gone wrong in talking of pleasure as though it were no more than contentment. Contentment consists roughly in relative absence of unsatisfied desires; pleasure is perhaps something more positive and consists in a balance between absence of unsatisfied desires and presence of satisfied desires. We might put the difference in this way: pure unconsciousness would be a limiting case of contentment, but not of pleasure. A stone has no unsatisfied desires, but then it just has no desires. Nevertheless, this consideration will not resolve the disagreement between Bentham and Mill. No doubt a dog has as intense a desire to discover rats as the philosopher has to discover the mysteries of the universe. Mill would wish to say that the pleasures of the philosopher were more valuable intrinsically than those of the dog, however intense these last might be. . . .

It is worth while enquiring how much practical ethics is likely to be affected by the possibility of disagreement over the question of Socrates dissatisfied versus the fool satisfied.

'Not very much,' one feels like saying at first. We noted that the most complex and intellectual pleasures are also the most fecund. Poetry elevates the mind, makes one more sensitive, and so harmonizes with various intellectual pursuits, some of which are of practical value. Delight in mathematics is even more obviously, on Benthamite views, a pleasure worth encouraging, for on the progress of mathematics depends the progress of mankind. Even the most hedonistic schoolmaster would prefer to see his boys enjoying poetry and mathematics rather than neglecting these arts for the pleasures of marbles or the tuckshop. Indeed many of the brutish pleasures not only lack fecundity but are actually the reverse of fecund. To enjoy food too much is to end up fat, unhealthy and without zest or vigour. To enjoy drink too much is even worse. In most circumstances of ordinary life the pure hedonist will agree in his practical recommendations with the quasi-ideal utilitarian.

This need not always be so. Some years ago two psychologists, Olds and Milner, carried out some experiments with rats. Through the skull of each rat they inserted an electrode. These electrodes penetrated to various regions of the brain. In the case of some of these regions the rat showed behaviour characteristics of pleasure when a current was passed from the electrode, in others they seemed to show pain, and in others the stimulus seemed neutral. That a stimulus was pleasure-giving was shown by the fact that the rat would learn to pass the current himself by pressing a lever. He would neglect food and make straight for this lever and start stimulating himself. In some cases he would sit there pressing the lever every few seconds for hours on end. This calls up a pleasant picture of the voluptuary of the future, a bald-headed man with a number of electrodes protruding from his skull, one to give the physical pleasure of sex, one for that of eating, one for that of drinking, and so on. Now is this the sort of life that all our ethical planning should culminate in? A few hours' work a week, automatic factories, comfort and security from disease, and hours spent at a switch, continually electrifying various regions of one's brain? Surely not. Men were made for higher things, one can't help wanting to say, even though one knows that men weren't made for anything, but are the product of evolution by natural selection.

It might be said that the objection to continual sensual stimulation of the above sort is that though it would be pleasant in itself it would be infecund of future pleasures. This is often so with the ordinary sensual pleasures. Excessive indulgence in the physical pleasures of sex may possibly have a debilitating effect and may perhaps interfere with the deeper feelings of romantic love. But whether stimulation by the electrode method would have this weakening effect and whether it would impair the possibility of future pleasures of the same sort is another matter. For example, there would be no excessive secretion of hormones. The whole biochemical mechanism would, almost literally, be short-circuited. Maybe, however, a person who stimulated himself by the electrode method would find it so enjoyable that he would neglect all other pursuits. Maybe if everyone became an electrode operator people would lose interest in everything else and the human race would die out.

Suppose, however, that the facts turned out otherwise: that a man could (and would) do his full share of work in the office or the factory and come back in the evening to a few hours contented electrode work, without bad after-effects. This would be his greatest pleasure, and the pleasure would be so great intrinsically and so easily repeatable that its lack of fecundity would not matter. Indeed perhaps by this time human arts, such as medicine, engineering, agriculture and architecture will have been brought to a pitch of perfection sufficient to enable most of the human race to spend most of its time electrode operating, without compensating pains of starvation, disease and squalor. Would this be a satisfactory state of society? Would this be the millennium towards which we have been striving? Surely the pure hedonist would have to say that it was.

It is time, therefore, that we had another look at the concept of happiness. Should we say that the electrode operator was really happy? This is a difficult question to be clear about, because the concept of happiness is a tricky one. But whether we should call the electrode operator 'happy' or not, there is no doubt (a) that he would be *contented* and (b) that he would be *enjoying himself*. . . .

. . . To call a person "happy" is to say more than that he is contented for most of the time, or even that he frequently enjoys himself and is rarely discontented or in pain. It is, I think, in part to express a favourable attitude to the idea of such a form of contentment and enjoyment. That is, for A to call B "happy," A must be contented at the prospect of B being in his present state of mind and at the prospect of A himself, should the opportunity arise, enjoying that sort of state of mind. That is, "happy" is a word which is mainly descriptive (tied to the concepts of contentment and enjoyment) but which is also partly evaluative. It is because Mill approves of the "higher" pleasures, e.g., intellectual pleasures, so much more than he approves of the more simple and brutish pleasures, that, quite apart from consequences and side effects, he can pronounce the man who enjoys the pleasures of philosophical discourse as "more happy" than the man who gets enjoyment from pushpin or beer drinking.

The word "happy" is not wholly evaluative, for there would be something absurd, as opposed to merely unusual, in calling a man who was in pain, or who was not enjoying himself, or who hardly ever enjoyed himself, or who was in a more or less permanent state of intense dissatisfaction, a "happy" man. For a man to be happy he must, as a minimal condition, be fairly contented and moderately enjoying himself for much of the time. Once this minimal condition is satisfied we can go on to evaluate various types of contentment and enjoyment and to grade them in terms of happiness. . . .

To sum up so far, happiness is partly an evaluative concept, and so the utilitarian maxim "You ought to maximize happiness" is doubly evaluative. There is the possibility of an ultimate disagreement between two utilitarians who differ over the question of pushpin versus poetry, or Socrates dissatisfied versus the fool satisfied. . . .

Leaving these more remote possibilities out of account, however, and considering the decisions we have to make at present, the question of whether the "higher" pleasures should be preferred to the "lower" ones does seem to be of slight practical importance. There are already perfectly good hedonistic arguments for poetry as against pushpin. As has been pointed out, the more complex pleasures are incomparably more fecund than the less complex ones: not only are they enjoyable in themselves but they are a means to further enjoyment. Still less, on the whole, do they lead to disillusionment, physical deterioration or social disharmony. The connoisseur of poetry may enjoy himself no more than the connoisseur of whisky, but he runs no danger of a headache on the following morning. Moreover the question of whether the general happiness would be increased by replacing most of the human population by a bigger population of contented sheep and pigs is not one which by any stretch of the imagination could become a live issue. Even if we thought, on abstract grounds, that such a replacement would be desirable, we should not have the slightest chance of having our ideas generally adopted. . . .

Another type of ultimate disagreement between utilitarians, whether hedonistic or ideal, can arise over whether we should try to maximize the *average* happiness of human beings (or the average goodness of their states of mind) or whether we should try to maximize the *total* happiness or goodness. . . . I have not yet elucidated the concept of total happiness, and you may regard it as a suspect notion. But for present purposes I shall put it in this way: Would you be quite indifferent between (a) a universe containing only one million happy sentient beings, all equally happy, and (b) a universe containing two million happy beings, each neither more nor less happy than any in the first universe? Or would you, as a humane and sympathetic person, give a preference to the second universe? I myself cannot help feeling a preference for the second universe. But if someone feels the other way I do not know how to argue with him. It looks as though we have yet another possibility of disagreement within a general utilitarian framework.

This type of disagreement might have practical relevance. It might be important in discussions of the ethics of birth control. This is not to say that the utilitarian who values total, rather than average, happiness may not have potent arguments in favour of birth control. But he will need more arguments to convince himself than will the other type of utilitarian.

In most cases the difference between the two types of utilitarianism will not lead to disagreement in practice. For in most cases the most effective way to increase the total happiness is to increase the average happiness, and vice versa. . . .

I shall now state the act-utilitarian doctrine. . . .

Let us say, then, that the only reason for performing an action A rather than an alternative action B is that doing A will make mankind (or, perhaps, all sentient beings) happier than will doing B. . . . This is so simple and natural a doctrine that we can surely expect that many of my readers will have at least some propensity to agree. For I am talking . . . to sympathetic and benevolent men, that is, to men who desire the happiness of mankind. Since they have a favourable attitude to the general happiness, surely they will have a tendency to submit to an ultimate moral principle which does no more than express this attitude. It is true that these men, being human, will also have purely selfish attitudes. Either these attitudes will be in harmony with the general happiness (in cases where everyone's looking after his own interests promotes the maximum general happiness) or they will not be in harmony with the general happiness, in which case they will largely cancel one another out, and so could not be made the basis of an interpersonal discussion anyway. It is possible, then, that many sympathetic and benevolent people depart from or fail to attain a utilitarian ethical principle only under the stress of tradition, of superstition, or of unsound philosophical reasoning. If this hypothesis should turn out to be correct, at least as far as these readers are concerned, then the utilitarian may contend that there is no need for him to defend his position directly, save by stating it in a consistent manner, and by showing that common objections to it are unsound. After all, it expresses an ultimate attitude, not a liking for something merely as a means to something else. Save for attempting to remove confusions and discredit superstitions which may get in the way of clear moral thinking, he cannot, of course, appeal to argument and must rest his hopes on the good feeling of his readers. If any reader is not a sympathetic and benevolent man, then of course it cannot be expected that he will have an ultimate pro-attitude to human happiness in general. Also some good-hearted readers may reject the utilitarian position because of certain considerations relating to justice. . . .

The utilitarian's ultimate moral principle, let it be remembered, expresses the sentiment not of altruism but of benevolence, the agent counting himself neither more nor less than any other person. Pure altruism cannot be made the basis of a universal moral discussion in that it would lead different people to different and perhaps incompatible courses of action, even though the circumstances were identical. When two men each try to let the other through a door first a deadlock results. Altruism could hardly commend itself to those of a scientific, and hence universalistic, frame of mind. If you count in my calculations why should I not count in your calculations? And why should I pay more attention to my calculations than to yours? Of course we often tend to praise and honour altrusim even more than generalized benevolence. This is because people too often err on the side of selfishness, and so altruism is a fault on the right side. If we can make a man try to be an altruist he may succeed as far as acquiring a generalized benevolence.

Suppose we could predict the future consequences of actions with certainty. Then it would be possible to say that the total future consequences of action A are such-and-such and that the total future consequences of action B are so-and-so. In order to help someone to decide whether to do A or to do B we could say to him: "Envisage the total consequences of A, and think them over carefully and imaginatively. Now envisage the total consequences of B, and think them over carefully. As a benevolent and humane man, and thinking of yourself just as one man among others, would you prefer the consequences of A or those of B?" That is, we are asking for a comparison of one (present and future) *total* situation with another (present and future) *total* situation. So far we are not asking for a *summation* or *calculation* of pleasures or happiness. We are asking only for a comparison of total situations. And it seems clear that we can frequently make such a comparison and say that one total situation is better than another. For example few people would not prefer a total situation in which a million people are well-fed, well-clothed, free of pain, doing interesting and enjoyable work, and enjoying the pleasures of conversation, study, business, art, humour, and so on, to a total situation where there are ten thousand such people only, or perhaps 999,999 such people plus one man with toothache, or neurotic, or shivering with cold. In general, we can sum things up by saying that if we are humane, kindly, benevolent people, we want as many people as possible now and in the future to be as happy as possible. Someone might object that we cannot envisage the total future situation, because this stretches into infinity. In reply to this we may say that it does not stretch into infinity, as all sentient life on earth will ultimately be extinguished, and furthermore we do not normally in practice need to consider very remote consequences, as these in the end approximate rapidly to zero like the furthermost ripples on a pond after a stone has been dropped into it.

But do the remote consequences of an action diminish to zero? Suppose that two people decide whether to have a child or remain childless. Let us suppose that they decide to have the child, and that they have a limitless succession of happy descendants. The remote consequences do not seem to get less. Not at any rate if these people are Adam and Eve. The difference would be between the end of the human race and a limitless accretion of human happiness, generation by generation. The Adam and Eve example shows that the "ripples on the pond" postulate is not needed in every case for a rational utilitarian decision. If we had some reason for thinking that every generation would be more happy than not we would not (in the Adam and Eve sort of case) need to be worried that the remote consequences of our action would be in detail unknown. The necessity for the "ripples in the pond" postulate comes from the fact that usually we do not know whether remote consequences will be good or bad. Therefore we cannot know what to do unless we can assume that remote consequences can be left out of account. This can often be done. Thus if we consider two actual parents, instead of Adam and Eve, then they need not worry about thousands of years hence. Not, at least, if we assume that there will be ecological forces determining the future population of the world. If these parents do not have remote descendants, then other people will presumably have more than they would otherwise. And there is no reason to suppose that my descendants would be more or less happy than yours. We must note, then, that unless we are dealing with "all or nothing" situations (such as the Adam and Eve one, or that of someone in a position to end human life altogether) we need some sort of "ripples in the pond" postulate to make utilitarianism workable in practice. I do not know how to prove such a postulate, though it seems plausible enough. If it is not accepted, not only utilitarianism, but also deontological systems like that of Sir David Ross, who at least admits beneficence as one *prima facie* duty among the others, will be fatally affected.

Sometimes, of course, more needs to be said. For example one course of action may make some people very happy and leave the rest as they are or perhaps slightly less happy. Another course of action may make all men rather more happy than before but no one very happy. Which course of action makes mankind happier on the whole? Again, one course of action may make it highly probable that everyone will be made a little happier whereas another course of action may give us a much smaller probability that everyone will be made very much happier. In the third place, one course of action may make everyone happy in a pig-like way, whereas another course of action may make a few people happy in a highly complex and intellectual way.

It seems therefore that we have to weigh the maximizing of happiness against equitable distribution, to weigh probabilities with happiness, and to weigh the intellectual and other qualities of states of mind with their pleasurableness. Are we not therefore driven back to the necessity of some calculus of happiness? Can we just say: "envisage two total situations and tell me which you prefer"? If this were possible, of course there would be no need to talk of summing happiness or of a calculus. All we should have to do would be to put total situations in an order of preference.

Let us now consider the question of equity. Suppose that we have the choice of sending four equally worthy and intelligent boys to a medium-grade public school or of leaving three in an adequate but uninspiring grammar school and sending one to Eton. (For sake of the example I am making the almost certainly incorrect assumption that Etonians are happier than other public-school boys and that these other public-school boys are happier than grammar-school boys.) Which course of action makes the most for the happiness of the four boys? Let us suppose that we can neglect complicating factors, such as that the superior Etonian education might lead one boy to develop his talents so much that he will have an extraordinary influence on the well-being of mankind, or that the unequal treatment of the boys might cause jealousy and rift in the family. Let us suppose that the Etonian will be as happy as (we may hope) Etonians usually are, and similarly for the other boys, and let us suppose that remote effects can be neglected. Should we prefer the greater happiness of one boy to the moderate happiness of all four? Clearly one parent may prefer one total situation (one boy at Eton and three at the grammar school) while another may prefer the other total situation (all four at the medium-grade public school). Surely both parents have an equal claim to being sympathetic and benevolent, and yet their difference of opinion here is not founded on an empirical disagreement about facts. I suggest, however, that there are not in fact many cases in which such a disagreement could arise. Probably the parent who wished to send one son to Eton would draw the line at sending one son to Eton plus giving him expensive private tuition during the holidays plus giving his other sons no secondary education at all. It is only within rather small limits that this sort of disagreement about equity can arise. Furthermore the cases in which we can make one person *very* much happier without increasing *general* happiness are rare ones. The law of diminishing returns comes in here. So, in most practical cases, a disagreement about what should be done will be an empirical disagreement about what total situation is likely to be brought about by an action, and will not be a disagreement about which total situation is preferable. For example the inequalitarian parent might get the other to agree with him if he could convince him that there was a much higher probability of an Etonian benefiting the human race, such as by inventing a valuable drug or opening up the mineral riches of Antarctica, than there is of a non-Etonian doing so. (Once more I should like to say that I do not myself take such a possibility very seriously!) I must again stress that since disagreement about what causes produce what effects is in practice so much the most important sort of disagreement, to have intelligent moral discussion with a person we do not in fact need complete agreement with him about ultimate ends: an approximate agreement is sufficient. . . .

According to the act-utilitarian, then, the rational way to decide what to do is to decide to perform that one of those alternative actions open to us (including the null-action, the doing of nothing) which is likely to maximize the probable happiness or well-being of humanity as a whole, or more accurately, of all sentient beings. The utilitarian position is here put forward as a criterion of rational choice. It is true that we may choose to habituate ourselves to behave in accordance with certain rules, such as to keep promises, in the belief that behaving in accordance with these rules is generally optimific, and in the knowledge that we most often just do not have time to work out individual pros and cons. When we act in such an habitual fashion we do not of course deliberate or make a choice. The act–utilitarian will, however, regard these rules as mere rules of thumb, and will use them only as rough guides. Normally he will act in accordance with them when he has no time for considering probable consequences or when the advantages of such a consideration of consequences are likely to be outweighed by the disadvantage of the waste of time involved. He acts in accordance with rules, in short, when there is no time to think, and since he does not think, the actions which he does habitually are not the outcome of moral thinking. When he has to think what to do, then there is a question of deliberation or choice, and it is precisely for such situations that the utilitarian criterion is intended.

It is, moreover, important to realize that there is no inconsistency whatever in an act–utilitarian's schooling himself to act, in normal circumstances, habitually and in accordance with stereotyped rules. He knows that a man about to save a drowning person has no time to consider various possibilities, such as that the drowning person is a dangerous criminal who will cause death and destruction, or that he is suffering from a painful and incapacitating disease from which death would be a merciful release, or that various timid people, watching from the bank, will suffer a heart attack if they see anyone else in the water. No, he knows that it is almost always right to save a drowning man, and in he goes. Again, he knows that we would go mad if we went in detail into the probable consequences of keeping or not keeping every trivial promise: we will do most good and reserve our mental energies for more important matters if we simply habituate ourselves to keep promises in all normal situations. Moreover he may suspect that on some occasions personal bias may prevent him from reasoning in a correct utilitarian fashion. . . .

Though even the act–utilitarian may on occasion act habitually and in accordance with particular rules, his criterion is, as we have said, *applied* in cases in which he does not act habitually but in which he deliberates and chooses what to do.

A Critique of
Utilitarianism

BERNARD WILLIAMS

Bernard Williams (b. 1929) is Knightbridge Professor of
Philosophy at the University of Cambridge. His books
include *Morality, Problems of the Self, Moral Luck,* and
Ethics and the Limits of Philosophy.

Williams's critique of consequentialism takes off from
Smart's version of act utilitarianism. If the consequences
are decisive in determining the right/wrongness of an
action, Williams says, then it will often be right to do
what is *prima facie* wrong. He presents two cases in
which, on utilitarian grounds, one would be forced to
act in a way that violated one's intuitive moral feelings.
In each case, "if the agent does not do a certain disagreeable thing, someone else will," and with much worse
consequences. The utilitarian holds that the agent must
then overcome his squeamishness and do the lesser evil.
In one of Williams's examples, a soldier, Pedro, will
shoot twenty innocent people unless a tourist, Jim,
shoots one of them. If Jim agrees, the remaining nineteen
will go free. Jim is naturally loath to commit murder,
but the consequences of his refusal to shoot will be much
worse. So far as the utilitarian is concerned, for Jim to
refrain from the murder is consequentially as bad as the
positive act of killing nineteen more people. This posi-

A CRITIQUE OF UTILITARIANISM   From "A Critique of Utilitarianism" in *Utilitarianism: For and
Against*, edited by J. J. C. Smart and Bernard Williams. Reprinted by permission of Cambridge
University Press.

tion, Williams argues, shows that utilitarianism has a confused notion of responsibility and a totally inadequate notion of personal integrity. If Jim refuses to kill one innocent person, he says, the responsibility for the deaths of the other nineteen is not Jim's but Pedro's. Williams points out that Jim's deepest convictions, projects, and attitudes "do not compute" in the utilitarian calculus: "How can a man, as a utilitarian agent, come to regard as one satisfaction among others, and a dispensable one, a project or attitude round which he has built his life, just because someone else's projects have so structured the causal scene that that is how the utilitarian sum comes out?"

It is perhaps worth mentioning that Bentham, at least, clearly separated the question of what action is objectively right in a given context from the quite different question of who, if anyone, should be held responsible.

. . . [L]et us look . . . at two examples to see what utilitarianism might say about them, what we might say about utilitarianism and, most importantly of all, what would be implied by certain ways of thinking about the situations. . . .

(1) George, who has just taken his Ph.D. in chemistry, finds it extremely difficult to get a job. He is not very robust in health, which cuts down the number of jobs he might be able to do satisfactorily. His wife has to go out to work to keep them, which itself causes a great deal of strain, since they have small children and there are severe problems about looking after them. The results of all this, especially on the children, are damaging. An older chemist, who knows about this situation, says that he can get George a decently paid job in a certain laboratory, which pursues research into chemical and biological warfare. George says that he cannot accept this, since he is opposed to chemical and biological warfare. The older man replies that he is not too keen on it himself, come to that, but after all George's refusal is not going to make the job or the laboratory go away; what is more, he happens to know that if George refuses the job, it will certainly go to a contemporary of George's who is not inhibited by any such scruples and is likely if appointed to push along the research with greater zeal than George

would. Indeed, it is not merely concern for George and his family, but (to speak frankly and in confidence) some alarm about this other man's excess of zeal, which has led the older man to offer to use his influence to get George the job . . . George's wife, to whom he is deeply attached, has views (the details of which need not concern us) from which it follows that at least there is nothing particularly wrong with research into CBW. What should he do?

(2) Jim finds himself in the central square of a small South American town. Tied up against the wall are a row of twenty Indians, most terrified, a few defiant, in front of them several armed men in uniform. A heavy man in a sweat-stained khaki shirt turns out to be the captain in charge and, after a good deal of questioning of Jim which establishes that he got there by accident while on a botanical expedition, explains that the Indians are a random group of the inhabitants who, after recent acts of protest against the government, are just about to be killed to remind other possible protestors of the advantages of not protesting. However, since Jim is an honoured visitor from another land, the captain is happy to offer him a guest's privilege of killing one of the Indians himself. If Jim accepts, then as a special mark of the occasion, the other Indians will be let off. Of course, if Jim refuses, then there is no special occasion, and Pedro here will do what he was about to do when Jim arrived, and kill them all. Jim, with some desperate recollection of schoolboy fiction, wonders whether if he got hold of a gun, he could hold the captain, Pedro and the rest of the soldiers to threat, but it is quite clear from the set-up that nothing of that kind is going to work: any attempt at that sort of thing will mean that all the Indians will be killed, and himself. The men against the wall, and the other villagers, understand the situation, and are obviously begging him to accept. What should he do?

To these dilemmas, it seems to me that utilitarianism replies, in the first case, that George should accept the job, and in the second, that Jim should kill the Indian. Not only does utilitarianism give these answers but, if the situations are essentially as described and there are no further special factors, it regards them, it seems to me, as *obviously* the right answers. But many of us would certainly wonder whether, in (1), that could possibly be the right answer at all; and in the case of (2), even one who came to think that perhaps that was the answer, might well wonder whether it was obviously the answer. Nor is it just a question of the rightness or obviousness

95

of these answers. It is also a question of what sort of considerations come into finding the answer. A feature of utilitarianism is that it cuts out a kind of consideration which for some others makes a difference to what they feel about such cases: a consideration involving the idea, as we might first and very simply put it, that each of us is specially responsible for what *he* does, rather than for what other people do. This is an idea closely connected with the value of integrity. It is often suspected that utilitarianism, at least in its direct forms, makes integrity as a value more or less unintelligible. I shall try to show that this suspicion is correct. . . .

. . . I want to consider now two types of effect that are often invoked by utilitarians, and which might be invoked in connexion with these imaginary cases. The attitude or tone involved in invoking these effects may sometimes seem peculiar; but that sort of peculiarity soon becomes familiar in utilitarian discussions, and indeed it can be something of an achievement to retain a sense of it.

First, there is the psychological effect on the agent. Our descriptions of these situations have not so far taken account of how George or Jim will be after they have taken the one course or the other; and it might be said that if they take the course which seemed at first the utilitarian one, the effects on them will be in fact bad enough and extensive enough to cancel out the initial utilitarian advantages of that course. Now there is one version of this effect in which, for a utilitarian, some confusion must be involved, namely that in which the agent feels bad, his subsequent conduct and relations are crippled and so on, *because he thinks that he has done the wrong thing*—for if the balance of outcomes was as it appeared to be *before* invoking this effect, then he has not (from the utilitarian point of view) done the wrong thing. So that version of the effect, for a rational and utilitarian agent, could not possibly make any difference to the assessment of right and wrong. However, perhaps he is not a thoroughly rational agent, and is disposed to have bad feelings, whichever he decided to do. Now such feelings, which are from a strictly utilitarian point of view irrational—nothing, a utilitarian can point out, is advanced by having them—cannot, consistently, have any great weight in a utilitarian calculation. I shall consider in a moment an argument to suggest that they should have no weight at all in it. But short of that, the utilitarian could reasonably say that such feelings should not be encouraged, even if we accept their existence, and that to give them a lot of weight is to

encourage them. Or, at the very best, even if they are straightfor-
wardly and without any discount to be put into the calculation,
their weight must be small: they are after all (and at best) one man's
feelings.

That consideration might seem to have particular force in Jim's
case. In George's case, his feelings represent a larger proportion of
what is to be weighed, and are more commensurate in character
with other items in the calculation. In Jim's case, however, his
feelings might seem to be of very little weight compared with other
things that are at stake. There is a powerful and recognizable appeal
that can be made on this point: as that a refusal by Jim to do what he
has been invited to do would be a kind of self-indulgent squeamishness. That is an appeal which can be made by other than utilitarians
—indeed, there are some uses of it which cannot be consistently
made by utilitarians, as when it essentially involves the idea that
there is something dishonourable about such self-indulgence. But
in some versions it is a familiar, and it must be said a powerful,
weapon of utilitarianism. One must be clear, though, about what it
can and cannot accomplish. The most it can do, so far as I can see, is
to invite one to consider how seriously, and for what reasons, one
feels that what one is invited to do is (in these circumstances)
wrong, and in particular, to consider that question from the utilitarian point of view. When the agent is not seeing the situation
from a utilitarian point of view, the appeal cannot force him to do
so; and if he does come round to seeing it from a utilitarian point of
view, there is virtually nothing left for the appeal to do. If he does
not see it from a utilitarian point of view, he will not see his
resistance to the invitation, and the unpleasant feelings he associates
with accepting it, *just* as disagreeable experiences of his; they figure
rather as emotional expressions of a thought that to accept would
be wrong. He may be asked, as by the appeal, to consider whether
he is right, and indeed whether he is fully serious, in thinking that.
But the assertion of the appeal, that he is being self-indulgently
squeamish, will not itself answer that question, or even help to
answer it, since it essentially tells him to regard his feelings just as
unpleasant experiences of his, and he cannot, by doing that, answer
the question they pose when they are precisely not so regarded, but
are regarded as indications of what he thinks is right and wrong. If
he does come round fully to the utilitarian point of view then of
course he will regard these feelings just as unpleasant experiences of

his. And once Jim—at least—has come to see them in that light, there is nothing left for the appeal to do, since *of course* his feelings, so regarded, are of virtually no weight at all in relation to the other things at stake. The 'squeamishness' appeal is not an argument which adds in a hitherto neglected consideration. Rather, it is an invitation to consider the situation, and one's own feelings, from a utilitarian point of view.

The reason why the squeamishness appeal can be very unsettling, and one can be unnerved by the suggestion of self-indulgence in going against utilitarian considerations, is not that we are utilitarians who are uncertain what utilitarian value to attach to our moral feelings, but that we are partially at least not utilitarians, and cannot regard our moral feelings merely as objects of utilitarian value. Because our moral relation to the world is partly given by such feelings, and by a sense of what we can or cannot 'live with,' to come to regard those feelings from a purely utilitarian point of view, that is to say, as happenings outside one's moral self, is to lose a sense of one's moral identity; to lose, in the most literal way, one's integrity. . . .

Integrity

The [two] situations have in common that if the agent does not do a certain disagreeable thing, someone else will, and in Jim's situation at least the result, the state of affairs after the other man has acted, if he does, will be worse than after Jim has acted, if Jim does. The same, on a smaller scale, is true of George's case. I have already suggested that it is inherent in consequentialism that it offers a strong doctrine of negative responsibility: if I know that if I do X, O_1 will eventuate, and if I refrain from doing X, O_2 will, and that O_2 is worse than O_1, then I am responsible for O_2 if I refrain voluntarily from doing X. 'You could have prevented it,' as will be said, and truly, to Jim, if he refuses, by the relatives of the other Indians. . . . [But] what occurs if Jim refrains from action is not solely twenty Indians dead, but *Pedro's killing twenty Indians.* . . . That may be enough for us to speak, in some sense, of Jim's responsibility for that outcome, if it occurs; but it is certainly not enough, it is worth noticing, for us to speak of Jim's *making* those things happen. For granted this way of their coming about, he could have made them happen only by making Pedro shoot, and there is no acceptable sense in which his refusal makes Pedro shoot. If the captain had said on Jim's refusal, 'you leave me with no alternative,' he would have been lying, like most who use that phrase. While the deaths, and the killing, may be the outcome of Jim's refusal, it is misleading to think, in such a case, of Jim having an *effect* on the world through the medium (as it happens) of Pedro's acts; for this is to leave Pedro out of the picture in his essential role of one who has intentions and projects, projects for realizing which Jim's refusal would leave an opportunity. Instead of thinking in terms of supposed effects of Jim's projects on Pedro, it is more revealing to think in terms of the effects of Pedro's projects on Jim's decision. . . .

Utilitarianism would do well . . . to acknowledge the evident fact that among the things that make people happy is not only making other people happy, but being taken up or involved in any of a vast range of projects, or—if we waive the evangelical and moralizing associations of the word—commitments. One can be committed to such things as a person, a cause, an institution, a career, one's own genius, or the pursuit of danger.

Now none of these is itself the *pursuit of happiness*: by an exceedingly ancient platitude, it is not at all clear that there could be anything which was just that, or at least anything that had the slightest chance of being successful. Happiness, rather, requires being involved in, or at least content with, something else. It is not impossible for utilitarianism to accept that point: it does not have to be saddled with a naïve and absurd philosophy of mind about the relation between desire and happiness. What it does have to say is that if such commitments are worth while, then pursuing the projects that flow from them, and realizing some of those projects, will make the person for whom they are worth while, happy. It may be that to claim that is still wrong: it may well be that a commitment can make sense to a man (can make sense of his life) without his supposing that it will make him *happy*. But that is not the present point; let us grant to utilitarianism that all worthwhile human projects must conduce, one way or another, to happiness. The point is that even if that is true, it does not follow, nor could it possibly be true, that those projects are themselves projects of pursuing happiness. One has to believe in, or at least want, or quite minimally, be content with, other things, for there to be anywhere that happiness can come from.

Utilitarianism, then, should be willing to agree that its general aim of maximizing happiness does not imply that what everyone is doing is just pursuing happiness. On the contrary, people have to be pursuing other things. What those other things may be, utilitarianism, sticking to its professed empirical stance, should be prepared just to find out. No doubt some possible projects it will want to discourage, on the grounds that their being pursued involves a negative balance of happiness to others: though even there, the unblinking accountant's eye of the strict utilitarian will have something to put in the positive column, the satisfactions of the destructive agent. Beyond that, there will be a vast variety of generally beneficent or at least harmless projects; and some no doubt, will take the form not just of tastes or fancies, but of what I have called 'commitments.' It may even be that the utilitarian researcher will find that many of those with commitments, who have really identified themselves with objects outside themselves, who are thoroughly involved with other persons, or institutions, or activities or causes, are actually happier than those whose projects and wants are not like that. If so, that is an important piece of utilitarian empirical lore.

When I say 'happier' here, I have in mind the sort of consideration which any utilitarian would be committed to accepting: as for instance that such people are less likely to have a break-down or commit suicide. Of course that is not all that is actually involved, but the point in this argument is to use to the maximum degree utilitarian notions, in order to locate a breaking point in utilitarian thought. In appealing to this strictly utilitarian notion, I am being more consistent with utilitarianism than Smart is. In his struggles with the problem of the brain-electrode man, Smart . . . commends the idea that 'happy' is a partly evaluative term, in the sense that we call 'happiness' those kinds of satisfaction which, as things are, we approve of. But *by what standard* is this surplus element of approval supposed, from a utilitarian point of view, to be allocated? There is no source for it, on a strictly utilitarian view, except further degrees of satisfaction, but there are none of those available, or the problem would not arise. Nor does it help to appeal to the fact that we dislike in prospect things which we like when we get there, for from a utilitarian point of view it would seem that the original dislike was merely irrational or based on an error. Smart's argument at this point seems to be embarrassed by a well-known utilitarian uneasiness, which comes from a feeling that it is not respectable to ignore the 'deep,' while not having anywhere left in human life to locate it.

On a utilitarian view . . . [t]he determination to an indefinite degree of my decisions by other people's projects is just another aspect of my unlimited responsibility to act for the best in a causal framework formed to a considerable extent by their projects.

The decision so determined is, for utilitarianism, the right decision. But what if it conflicts with some project of mine? This, the utilitarian will say, has already been dealt with: the satisfaction to you of fulfilling your project, and any satisfaction to others of your so doing, have already been through the calculating device and have been found inadequate. Now in the case of many sorts of projects, that is a perfectly reasonable sort of answer. But in the case of projects of the sort I have called 'commitments,' those with which one is more deeply and extensively involved and identified, this cannot just by itself be an adequate answer, and there may be no adequate answer at all. For, to take the extreme sort of case, how can a man, as a utilitarian agent, come to regard as one satisfaction among others, and a dispensable one, a project or attitude round which he has built his life, just because someone else's projects have so structured the causal scene that that is how the utilitarian sum comes out?

The point here is not, as utilitarians may hasten to say, that if the project or attitude is that central to his life, then to abandon it will be very disagreeable to him and great loss of utility will be involved. . . . On the contrary, once he is prepared to look at it like that, the argument in any serious case is over anyway. The point is that he is identified with his actions as flowing from projects and attitudes which in some cases he takes seriously at the deepest level, as what his life is about (or, in some cases, this section of his life—seriousness is not necessarily the same as persistence). It is absurd to demand of such a man, when the sums come in from the utility network which the projects of others have in part determined, that he should just step aside from his own project and decision and acknowledge the decision which utilitarian calculation requires. It is to alienate him in a real sense from his actions and the source of his action in his own convictions. It is to make him into a channel between the input of everyone's projects, including his own, and an output of optimific decision; but this is to neglect the extent to which *his* actions and *his* decisions have to be seen as the actions and decisions which flow from the projects and attitudes with which he is most closely identified. It is thus, in the most literal sense, an attack on his integrity.

[T]he immediate point of all this is to draw one particular contrast with utilitarianism: that to reach a grounded decision . . . should not be regarded as a matter of just discontinuing one's reactions, impulses and deeply held projects in the face of the pattern of utilities, nor yet merely adding them in—but in the first instance of trying to understand them.

Of course, time and circumstances are unlikely to make a grounded decision, in Jim's case at least, possible. Very often, we just act, as a possibly confused result of the situation in which we are engaged. That, I suspect, is very often an exceedingly good thing.

Rule-Utilitarianism

JOHN HOSPERS

John Hospers (b. 1918) is the director of the School of Philosophy at the University of Southern California. He is the author of a number of books, including *Libertarianism: A Political Philosophy for Tomorrow* and *Understanding the Arts*. He ran for president of the United States in 1972 on the Libertarian ticket.

Hospers takes up the question—also dealt with by Smart—of how to justify obeying rules ("Do not cheat"; "Everyone should vote") when breaking them seems preferable on utilitarian grounds. For example, why shouldn't teachers make students happy by some-

RULE-UTILITARIANISM Excerpted from *Human Conduct: An Introduction to the Problem of Ethics* by John Hospers, copyright © 1961 by Harcourt Brace Jovanovich, Inc. Reprinted by permission of the publisher.

times giving them better grades than they deserve? Why not send a guilty criminal to prison on false evidence? More generally, why not break the rules if that will do the most good? Hospers argues for rule-utilitarianism, which he calls a "twentieth-century amendment of the utilitarianism of Bentham and Mill, . . . called *act-utilitarianism*." Making exceptions to rules is bad practice and poor policy on utilitarian grounds, he says. Kant's principle that any rule possessing moral authority must be one we want to see universally applied is in this way shared by rule-utilitarianism. Hospers ends his article by showing how the rule-utilitarian can help us to avoid "universalizing" silly rules that are either too general ("Don't kill except when it will do the most good") or too specific ("Never lie on Tuesday afternoon").

1. In order to receive a high enough grade average to be admitted to medical school, a certain student must receive either an A or a B in one of my courses. After his final examination is in, I find, on averaging his grades, that his grade for the course comes out to a C. The student comes into my office and begs me to change the grade, on the ground that I have not read his paper carefully enough. So I reread his final exam paper, as well as some of the other papers in the class in order to get a better sense of comparison; the rechecking convinces me that his grade should be no higher than the one I have given him—if anything, it should be lower. I inform him of my opinion and he still pleads with me to change the grade, but for a different reason. "I know I didn't deserve more than a C, but I appeal to you as a human being to change my grade, because without it I can't get into medical school, which naturally means a great deal to me." I inform him that grades are supposed to be based on achievement in the course, not on intentions or need or the worthiness of one's plans. But he pleads: "I know it's unethical to change a grade when the student doesn't deserve a higher one, but can't you please make an exception to the rule just this once?" And before I can reply, he sharpens his plea: "I appeal to you as a utilitarian. Your goal is the greatest happiness of everyone concerned, isn't it? If you give me only the grade I deserve, who will be

happier? Not I, that's sure. Perhaps you will for a little while, but you have hundreds of students and you'll soon forget about it; and I will be ever so much happier for being admitted into a school that will train me for the profession I have always desired. It's true that I didn't work as hard in your course as I should have, but I realize my mistake and I wouldn't waste so much time if I had it to do over again. Anyway, you should be forward-looking rather than backward-looking in your moral judgments, and there is no doubt whatever that much more happiness will be caused (and unhappiness prevented) by your giving me the higher grade even though I fully admit that I don't deserve it."

After pondering the matter, I persist in believing that it would not be right to change the grade under these circumstances. Perhaps you agree with my decision and perhaps you don't, but *if* you agree that I should not have changed the grade, and *if* you are also a utilitarian, how are you going to reconcile such a decision with utilitarianism? *Ex hypothesi*, the greatest amount of happiness will be brought about by my changing the grade, so why shouldn't I change it?

Of course, if I changed the grade and went around telling people about it, my action would tend to have an adverse effect on the whole system of grading—and this system is useful to graduate schools and future employers to give some indication of the student's achievement in his various courses. But of course if I tell no one, nobody will know, and my action cannot set a bad example to others. This in turn raises an interesting question: If it is wrong for me to do the act publicly, is it any the less wrong for me to do it secretly?

2. A man is guilty of petty theft and is sentenced to a year in prison. Suppose he can prove to the judge's satisfaction that he would be happier out of jail, that his wife and family would too (they depend on his support), that the state wouldn't have the expense of his upkeep if he were freed, and that people won't hear about it because his case didn't hit the papers and nobody even knows that he was arrested—in short, everyone concerned would be happier and nobody would be harmed by his release. And yet, we feel, or at least many people would, that to release him would be a mistake. The sentence imposed on him is the minimum permitted by law for his offense, and he should serve out his term in accordance with the law.

3. A district attorney who has prosecuted a man for robbery chances upon information which shows conclusively that the man he has prosecuted is innocent of the crime for which he has just been sentenced. The man is a wastrel who, if permitted to go free, would almost certainly commit other crimes. Moreover, the district attorney has fairly conclusive evidence of the man's guilt in prior crimes, for which, however, the jury has failed to convict him. Should he, therefore, "sit on the evidence" and let the conviction go through in this case, in which he knows the man to be innocent? We may not be able to articulate exactly *why*, but we feel strongly that the district attorney should not sit on the evidence but that he should reveal every scrap of evidence he knows, even though the revelation means releasing the prisoner (now known to be innocent) to do more crimes and be convicted for them later.

X: It seems to me that some acts are right or wrong, not *regardless* of the consequences they produce, but *over and above* the consequences they produce. We would all agree, I suppose, that you should break a promise to save a life but not that you should break it whenever you considered it probable (even with good reason) that more good effects will come about through breaking it. Suppose you had promised someone you would do something and you didn't do it. When asked why, you replied, "Because I thought breaking it would have better results." Wouldn't the promisee condemn you for your action, and rightly? This example is quite analogous, I think, to the example of the district attorney; the district attorney might argue that more total good will be produced by keeping the prisoner's innocence secret. Besides, if he is released, people may read about it in the newspaper and say, "You see, you can get by with anything these days" and may be encouraged to violate the law themselves as a result. Still, even though it would do more total good if the man were to remain convicted, wouldn't it be wrong to do so in view of the fact that he is definitely innocent of *this* crime? The law punishes a man, not necessarily because the most good will be achieved that way, but because he has committed a crime; if we don't approve of the law, we can do our best to have it changed, but meanwhile aren't we bound to follow it? Those who execute the law are sworn to obey it; they are *not* sworn to produce certain consequences.

Y: Yes, but remember that the facts *might* always come out after their concealment and that we can never be sure they won't. If they do, keeping the man in prison will be far worse than letting the man go; it will result in a great public distrust for the law itself; nothing is more demoralizing than corruption of the law by its own supposed enforcers. Better let a hundred human derelicts go free than risk that! You see, *one* of the consequences you always have to consider is the effect of *this* action on the *general practice* of law-breaking itself; and when you bring in *this* consequence, it will surely weigh the balance in favor of divulging the information that will release the innocent man. So utilitarianism will still account quite satisfactorily for this case. I agree that the man should be released, but I do so on utilitarian grounds; I needn't abandon my utilitarianism at all to take care of this case.

X: But your view is open to one fatal objection. You say that one never can be sure that the news *won't* leak out. Perhaps so. But suppose that in a given case one *could* be sure; would that really make any difference? Suppose you are the only person that knows and you destroy the only existing evidence. Since you are not going to talk, there is simply no chance that the news will leak out, with consequent damage to public morale. Then is it all right to with-hold the information? You see, I hold that if it's wrong not to reveal the truth when others might find out, then it's equally wrong not to reveal it when *nobody* will find out. You utilitarians are involved in the fatal error of making the rightness or wrongness of an act depend on whether performing it will ever be publicized. And I hold that it is immoral even to consider this condition; the district attorney should reveal the truth regardless of whether his conceal-ing it would ever be known.

Y: But surely you aren't saying that one should *never* conceal the truth? not even if your country is at war against a totalitarian enemy and revealing truths to the people would also mean reveal-ing them to the enemy?

X: Of course I'm not saying that—don't change the subject. I am saying that *if* in situation S it is wrong to convict an innocent man, then it is equally wrong whether or not the public knows that it is wrong; the public's knowledge will certainly have bad con-sequences, but the conviction would be wrong anyway even *with-out* these bad consequences; so you can't appeal to the consequences of the conviction's becoming public as grounds for saying that the conviction is wrong. I think that you utilitarians are really stuck here. For you, the consideration "but nobody is ever going to know about it anyway" is a relevant consideration. It has to be; for the rightness of an act (according to you) is estimated in terms of its total consequences, and its total consequences, of course, include its effects (or lack of effects) on other acts of the same kind, and there won't be any such effects if the act is kept absolutely secret. You have to consider *all* the consequences relevant; the matter of keeping the thing quiet is one consequence; so you have to consider this one relevant too. Yet I submit to you that it isn't relevant; the suggestion "but nobody is going to know about it anyway" is not one that will help make the act permissible if it wasn't before. If anything, it's the other way round: something bad that's done publicly and openly is not as bad as if it's done secretly so as to escape detection; secret sins are the worst. . . .

Y: I deny what you say. It seems to me worse to betray a trust in public, where it may set an example to others, than to do so in secret, where it can have no bad effects on others.

X: And I submit that you would never say that if you weren't already committed to the utilitarian position. Here is a situation where you and practically everyone else would not hesitate to say that an act done in secret is no less wrong than when done in public, were it not that it flies in the face of a doctrine to which you have already committed yourself on the basis of quite different examples.

4. Here is a still different kind of example. We consider it our duty in a democracy to vote and to do so wisely and intelligently as possible, for only if we vote wisely can a democracy work successfully. But in a national election my vote is only one out of millions, and it is more and more improbable that *my* vote will have any effect upon the outcome. Nor is my failure to vote going to affect other people much, if at all. Couldn't a utilitarian argue this way: "My vote will have no effect at all—at least far, far less than other things I could be doing instead. Therefore, I shall not vote." Each and every would-be voter could argue in exactly the same way. The result would be that nobody would vote, and the entire democratic process would be destroyed.

What conclusion emerges from these examples? If the examples point at all in the right direction, they indicate that there are some acts which it is right to perform, even though by themselves they will not have good consequences (such as my voting), and that there are some acts which it is wrong to perform, even though by themselves they would have good consequences (such as sitting on the evidence). But this conclusion is opposed to utilitarianism as we have considered it thus far. . . .

Rule-Utilitarianism and Objections to It

The batter swings, the ball flies past, the umpire yells "Strike three!" The disappointed batter pleads with the umpire, "Can't I have four strikes just this once?" We all recognize the absurdity of this example. Even if the batter could prove to the umpire's satisfaction that he would be happier for having four strikes this time, that the spectators would be happier for it (since most of the spectators are on his side), that there would be little dissatisfaction on the side of the opposition (who might have the game clinched anyway), and that there would be no effect on future baseball games, we would still consider his plea absurd. We might think, "Perhaps baseball would be a better game—i.e., contribute to the greatest total enjoyment of all concerned—if four strikes were permitted. If so, we should change the rules of the game. But until that time, we must play baseball according to the rules which are now the accepted rules of the game."

This example, though only an analogy, gives us a clue to the kind of view we are about to consider—let us call it *rule-utilitarianism*. Briefly stated (we shall amplify it gradually), rule-utilitarianism comes to this: Each act, in the moral life, falls under a *rule*; and we are to judge the rightness or wrongness of the act, not by *its* consequences, but by the consequences of its universalization—that is, by the consequences of the adoption of the *rule* under which this act falls. This . . . interpretation of Kant's categorical imperative . . . differs from Kant in being concerned with consequences, but retains the main feature which Kant introduced, that of universalizability.

Thus: The district attorney may do more good in a particular case by sitting on the evidence, but even if this case has no consequences for future cases because nobody ever finds out, still, the general policy or *practice* of doing this kind of thing is a very bad one; it uproots one of the basic premises of our legal system, namely that an innocent person should not be condemned. Our persistent conviction that it would be wrong for him to conceal the evidence in this case comes *not* from the conviction that concealing the evidence will produce less good—we may be satisfied that it will produce more good in this case—but from the conviction that the *practice* of doing this kind of thing will have very bad consequences. In other words, "Conceal the evidence when you think that it will produce more happiness" would be a bad rule to follow, and it is because this *rule* (if adopted) would have bad consequences, not because *this* act itself has bad consequences, that we condemn the act.

The same applies in other situations: . . . perhaps I can achieve more good, in this instance, by changing the student's grade, but the consequences of the general practice of changing students' grades for such reasons as these would be very bad indeed; a graduate school or a future employer would no longer have reason to believe that the grade-transcript of the student had any reference to his real achievement in his courses; he would wonder how many of the high grades resulted from personal factors like pity, need, and irrelevant appeals by the student to the teacher. The same considerations apply also to the voting example: if Mr. Smith can reason that his vote won't make any difference to the outcome, so can Mr. Jones and Mr. Robinson and every other would-be voter; but if everyone reasoned in this way, no one would vote, and this *would* have bad effects. It is considered one's duty to vote, not because the consequences of one's not doing so are bad, but because the consequences of the general practice of not doing so are bad. To put it in Kantian language, the maxim of the action, if universalized, would have bad consequences. But the individual act of *your* not voting on a specific occasion—or of any *one* person's not voting, as long as *others* continued to vote—would probably have no bad consequences.

There are many other examples of the same kind of thing. If during a water shortage there is a regulation that water should not be used to take baths every day or to water gardens, there will be virtually no bad consequences if only *I* violate the rule. Since there will be no discernible difference to the city water supply and since my plants will remain green and fresh and pleasant to look at, why shouldn't I water my plants? But if everyone watered his plants, there would not be enough water left to drink. My act is judged wrong, not because of *its* consequences, but because the consequences of everyone doing so would be bad. If I walk on the grass where the sign says, "Do not walk on the grass," there will be no ill effects; but if everyone did so it would destroy the grass. There are some kinds of act which have little or no effect if any one person (or two, or three) does them but which have very considerable effects if everyone (or even just a large number) does them. Rule-utilitarianism is designed to take care of just such situations.

Rule-utilitarianism also takes care of situations which are puzzling in traditional utilitarianism, . . . namely, the secrecy with which an act is performed. "But no one will ever know, so my act won't have any consequences for future acts of the same kind," the utilitarian argued; and we felt that he was being somehow irrelevant, even immoral: that if something is wrong when people know about it, it is just as wrong when done in secret. Yet this condition *is* relevant according to traditional utilitarianism, for if some act with bad consequences is never known to anyone, this ignorance does mitigate the bad consequences, for it undeniably keeps the act from setting an example (except, of course, that it may start a habit in the agent himself). Rule-utilitarianism solves this difficulty. If I change the student's grade in secret, my act is wrong, in spite of its having almost no consequences (and never being known to anyone else), because if I change the grade and don't tell anyone, how do I know how many other teachers are changing their students' grades without telling anybody? It is the result of the *practice* which is bad, not the result of my single action. The result of the practice is bad whether the act is done in secret or not: the result of the practice of changing grades in secret is just as bad as the results of the practice done in full knowledge of everyone; it would be equally deleterious to the grading system, equally a bad index of a student's actual achievement. In fact, if changing grades is done in secret, this in one way is worse; for prospective employers will not know, as they surely ought to know in evaluating their prospective employees, that their grades are not based on achievement but on other factors such as poverty, extra-curricular work load, and persuasive appeal.

Rule utilitarianism is a distinctively twentieth-century amendment of the utilitarianism of Bentham and Mill, often called *act-utilitarianism*. . . . Since this pair of labels is brief and indicates clearly the contents of the theories referred to, we prefer these terms to a second pair of labels, which are sometimes used for the same theories: *restricted utilitarianism* as opposed to *unrestricted* (or extreme, or *traditional*) *utilitarianism*. (Whether or not Mill's theory is strictly act-utilitarianism is a matter of dispute. Mill never made the distinction between act-utilitarianism and rule-utilitarianism. . . . Some of Mill's examples, however, have to do not with individual acts but with general principles and rules of conduct. Mill and Bentham were both legislators, interested in amending the laws of England into greater conformity to the utilitarian principle; and to the extent that Mill was interested in providing a criterion of judging rules of conduct rather than individual acts, he may be said to have been a rule-utilitarian.)

Much more must be said before the full nature of the rule-utilitarian theory becomes clear. To understand it better, we shall consider some possible questions, comments, and objections that can be put to the theory as thus far stated.

1. Doesn't the . . . problem arise here . . . of *what* precisely we are to universalize? Every act can be put into a vast variety of classes of acts; or, in our present terminology, every act can be made to fall under many different general rules. Which rule among this vast variety are we to select? We can pose our problem by means of an imaginary dialogue referring back to Kant's ethics and connecting it with rule-utilitarianism:

A: Whatever may be said for Kant's ethics in general, there is one principle of fundamental importance which must be an indispensable part of every ethics—the principle of universalizability. If some act is right for me to do, it would be right for all rational beings to do it; and if it is wrong for them to do it, it would be wrong for me too.

B: If this principle simply means that nobody should make an exception in his own favor, the principle is undoubtedly true and is psychologically important in view of the fact that people constantly do make exceptions in their own favor. But as it stands I can't follow you in agreeing with Kant's principle. Do you mean that if it is wrong for Smith to get a divorce, it is also wrong for Jones to do so? But this isn't so. Smith may be hopelessly incompatible with his wife, and they may be far better off apart, whereas Jones may be reconcilable with his wife (with some mutual effort) and a divorce in his case would be a mistake. Each case must be judged on its own merits.

A: The principle doesn't mean that if it's right for one person, A, to do it, it is therefore right for B and C and D to do it. It means that if it's right for one person to do it, it is right for anyone *in those*

111

circumstances to do it. And Jones isn't in the same circumstances as Smith. Smith and his wife would be better off apart, and Jones and his wife would be better off together.

B: I see. Do you mean *exactly* the same circumstances or *roughly* the same (similar) circumstances?

A: I think I would have to mean exactly the same circumstances for if the circumstances were not quite alike, that little difference might make the difference between a right act (done by Smith) and a wrong act (done by Jones). For instance, if in Smith's case there are no children and in Jone's case there are, this fact may make a difference.

B: Right. But I must urge you to go even further. Two men might be in exactly the same *external* circumstances, but owing to their *internal constitution* what would be right for one of them wouldn't be for the other. Jones may have the ability to be patient, impartial, and approach problems rationally, and Smith may not have this ability; here again is a relevant difference between them, although not a difference in their external circumstances. Or: Smith, after he reaches a certain point of fatigue, would do well to go fishing for a few days—this would refresh and relax him as nothing else could. But Jones dislikes fishing; it tries and irritates and bores him; so even if he were equally tired and had an equally responsible position, he would not be well advised to go fishing. Or again: handling explosives might be all right for a trained intelligent person, but not for an ignorant blunderbuss. In the light of such examples as these, you see that under the "same circumstances" you'll have to include not only the external circumstances in which they find themselves but their own internal character.

A: I grant this. So what?

B: But now your universalizability principle becomes useless. For two people never *are* in exactly the same circumstances. Nor can they be: if Smith were in exactly the same circumstances as Jones, including all his traits of character, his idiosyncracies, and his brain cells, he would *be* Jones. You see, your universalizability principle is inapplicable. It would become applicable only under conditions (two people being the same person) which are self-contradictory,—and even if not self-contradictory, you'll have to admit that two exactly identical situations never occur; so once again the rule is inapplicable.

A: I see your point; but I don't think I need go along with your conclusion. Smith and Jones should do the same thing only if their situation or circumstances are the same in certain *relevant respects*. The fact that Jones is wearing a white shirt and Smith a blue one, is a difference of circumstances, but, surely, an *irrelevant* difference, a difference that for moral purposes can be ignored. But the fact that Smith and his wife are emotionally irreconcilable while Jones and his wife could work things out, would be a morally relevant circumstance.

B: Possibly. But how are you going to determine which differences are relevant and which are not?

Kant . . . never solved this problem. He assumed that "telling a lie" was morally relevant but that "telling a lie to save a life" was not; but he gave no reason for making this distinction. The rule-utilitarian has an answer.

Suppose that a red-headed man with one eye and a wart on his right cheek tells a lie on a Tuesday. What rule are we to derive from this event? Red-headed men should not tell lies? People shouldn't lie on Tuesdays? Men with warts on their cheeks shouldn't tell lies on Tuesdays? These rules seem absurd, for it seems so obvious that whether it's Tuesday or not, whether the man has a wart on his cheek or not, has nothing whatever to do with the rightness of his action—these circumstances are just *irrelevant*. But this is the problem: how are we going to establish this irrelevance? What is to be our criterion?

The criterion we tried to apply . . . was to make the rule more *specific*: instead of saying, "This is a lie and is therefore wrong," . . . we made it more specific and said, "This is a lie told to save a life and is therefore right." We could make the rule more specific still, involving the precise circumstances in which this lie is told, other than the fact that it is told to save a life. But, now it seems, the use of greater specificity will not always work: instead of "Don't tell lies," suppose we say, "Don't tell lies on Tuesdays." The second is certainly more specific than the first, but is it a better rule? It seems plain that it is not—that its being a Tuesday is, in fact, wholly irrelevant. Why?

"Because," says the rule-utilitarian, "there is no difference between the effects of lies told on Tuesdays and the effects of lies told on any other day. This is simply an empirical fact, and because of this empirical fact, bringing in Tuesday is irrelevant. If lies told on Tuesdays always had good consequences and lies told on other days were disastrous, then a lie's being told on a Tuesday would be relevant to the moral estimation of the act; but in fact this is not true. Thus there is no advantage in specifying the subclass of lies, 'lies told on Tuesdays.' The same is true of 'lies told by redheads' and 'lies told by persons with warts on their cheeks.' The class of lies can be made more specific—that is no problem—but not more *relevantly* specific, at least not in the direction of Tuesdays and redheads. (However, the class can be made more relevantly specific considering certain other aspects of the situation, such as whether the lie was told to produce a good result that could not have been brought about otherwise.)"

Consider by contrast a situation in which the class of acts can easily be made relevantly more specific. A pacifist might argue as follows: "I should never use physical violence in any form against another human being, since if everyone refrained from violence, we would have a warless world." There are aspects of this example that we cannot discuss now, but our present concern with it is as follows. We can break down violence into more specific types such as violence which is unprovoked, violence in defense of one's life against attack by another, violence by a policeman in catching a lawbreaker, violence by a drunkard in response to an imaginary affront. The effects of these subclasses of violence do differ greatly in their effects upon society. Violence used by a policeman in apprehending a lawbreaker (at least under some circumstances, which could be spelled out) and violence used in preventing a would be murderer from killing you, do on the whole have good effects; but the unprovoked violence of an aggressor or a drunkard does not. Since these subclasses do have different effects, therefore, it *is* relevant to consider them. Indeed, it is imperative to do so: the pacifist who condemns *all* violence would probably, if he thought about it, not wish to condemn the policeman who uses violent means to prevent an armed madman from killing a dozen people. In any event, the effects of the two subclasses of acts are vastly different; and, the rule-utilitarian would say, it is accordingly very important for us to consider them—to break down the general class of violent acts into more specific classes and consider separately the effects of each one until we have arrived at subclasses which cannot *relevantly* be made more specific.

How specific shall we be? Won't we get down to "acts of violence to prevent aggression, performed on Tuesdays at 11:30 P.M.

in hot weather" and subclasses of that sort? And aren't these again plainly irrelevant? Of course they are, and the reason has already been given: acts of violence performed on Tuesdays, or at 11:30 P.M., or by people with blue suits, are no different in their effects from acts-of-violence-to-prevent-aggression done in circumstances other than these; and therefore these circumstances, though more specific, are not relevantly more specific. When the consequences of these more specific classes of acts differ from the consequences of the more general class, it is this specific class which should be considered; but when the consequences of the specific classes are not different from those of the more general class, the greater specificity is irrelevant and can be ignored.

The rule, then, is this: we should consider the consequences of the general performance of certain classes of actions only if that class contains within itself no subclasses, the consequences of the general practice of which would be either better or worse than the consequences of the class itself.

Let us take an actual example of how this rule applies. Many people, including Kant, have taken the principle "Thou shalt not kill" as admitting of no exceptions. But as we have just seen, such principles can be relevantly made more specific. Killing for fun is one thing, killing in self-defense another. Suppose, then, that we try to arrive at a general rule on which to base our actions in this regard. We shall try to arrive at that rule the general following of which will have the best results. Not to kill an armed bandit who is about to shoot you if you don't shoot him first, would appear to be a bad rule by utilitarian standards; for it would tend to eliminate the good people and preserve the bad ones; moreover, if nobody resisted aggressors, the aggressors, knowing this, would go hog-wild and commit indiscriminate murder, rape, and plunder. Therefore, "Don't kill except in self-defense" (though we might improve this rule too) would be a better rule than "Never kill." But "Don't kill unless you feel angry at the victim" would be a bad rule, because the adoption of this rule would lead to no end of indiscriminate killing for no good reason. The trick is to arrive at the rule which, if adopted, would have the very best possible consequences (which includes, of course, the absolute minimum of bad consequences). Usually no simple or easily statable rule will do this, the world being as complex as it is. There will usually be subclasses of classes-of-acts which are relevantly more specific than the simple, general class with which we began. And even when we think we have arrived at a satisfactory rule, there always remains the possibility that it can relevantly be made more specific, and thus amended, with an increase in accuracy but a consequent decrease in simplicity.

To a considerable extent most people recognize this complexity. Very few people would accept the rule against killing without some qualifications. However much they may preach and invoke the rule "Thou shall not kill" in situations where it happens to suit them, they would never recommend its adoption in all circumstances: when one is defending himself against an armed killer, almost everyone would agree that killing is permissible, although he may not have formulated any theory from which this exception follows as a logical consequence. Our practical rule against killing contains within itself (often not explicitly stated) certain *classes of exceptions*: "Don't kill *except* in self-defense, in war against an aggressor nation, in carrying out the verdict of a jury recommending capital punishment." This would be a far better rule—judged by its consequences—than any simple one-line rule on the subject. Each of the classes of exceptions could be argued pro and con, of course. But such arguments would be empirical ones, hinging on whether or not the adoption of such classes of exceptions into the rule would have the maximum results in intrinsic good. (Many would argue, for example, that capital punishment achieves no good effects; on the other hand, few would contend that the man who pulls the switch at Sing Sing is committing a crime in carrying out the orders of the legal representatives of the state.) And there may always be other kinds of situations that we have not previously thought of, situations which, if incorporated into the rule, would improve the rule—that is, make it have better consequences; and thus the rule remains always open, always subject to further qualification if the addition of such qualification would improve the rule.

These qualifications of the rule are not, strictly speaking, *exceptions to* the rule. According to rule-utilitarianism, the rule, once fully stated, admits of no exceptions; but there may be, and indeed there usually are, numerous classes of exceptions *built into the* rule; a simple rule becomes through qualification a more complex rule. Thus, if a man kills someone in self-defense and we do not consider his act wrong, we are not making him an exception to the rule. Rather, his act *falls under* the rule—the rule that includes killing in self-defense as one of the classes of acts which is permissible (or, if you prefer, the rule that includes self-defense as one of the circumstances in which the rule against killing does not apply). Similarly, if a man parks in a prohibited area and the judge does not fine him because he is a physician making a professional call, the judge is not extending any favoritism to the physician; he is not making the physician an exception to the rule; rather, the rule (though it may not always be written out in black and white) includes within itself this recognized class of exceptions—or, more accurately still, the rule includes within itself a reference to just this kind of situation, so that the action of the judge in exonerating the physician is just as much an application of the rule (not an exception to it) as another act of the same judge in imposing a fine on someone else for the same offense.

We can now see how our previous remarks about acts committed in secret fit into the rule-utilitarian scheme. On the one hand, the rule "Don't break a promise except (1) under extreme duress and (2) to promote some very great good" is admittedly somewhat vague, and perhaps it could be improved by still further qualification; but at least it is much better than the simple rule "Never break promises." On the other hand, the rule "Don't break a promise except when nobody will know about it" is a bad rule: there are many situations in which keeping promises is important . . . situations in which promises could not be relied on if this rule were adopted. That is why, among the circumstances which excuse you from keeping your word, the fact that it was broken in secret is not one of them—and for a very good reason: if this class of exceptions were incorporated into the rule, the rule's adoption would have far worse effects than if it did not contain such a clause. . . .

Rule-utilitarianism and act-utilitarianism are alike with regard to relativism. They are *not* relativistic in that they have one standard, one "rule of rules," one supreme norm, applicable to all times and situations: "Perform that act which will produce the most intrinsic good" (act-utilitarianism), "Act according to the rule whose adoption will produce the most intrinsic good" (rule-utilitarianism). But within the scope of that one standard, the recommended rules of conduct may well vary greatly from place to place. . . . In a desert area the act of wasting water will cause much harm and is therefore wrong, but it is not wrong in a region where water is plentiful. In a society where men and women are approximately equal in number, it will be best for a husband to have only one wife; but in a society in which there is great numerical disparity between the two, this arrangement may no longer be wise. So much for act-utilitarianism; the same goes for rule-utilitarianism. The rule "Never waste water" is a good rule, indeed an indispensable rule, in a desert region but not in a well-watered region. Monogamy seems to be the best possible marital system in our society but not necessarily in all societies—it depends on the conditions. What are the best acts and the best rules at a given time and place, then, depends on the special circumstances of that time and place. Some conditions, of course, are so general that the rules will be much the same everywhere: a rule against killing (at least within the society) is an indispensable condition of security and survival and therefore must be preserved in all societies.

The situation, then, is this: Rule or Act A is right in circumstances C_1, and rule or Act B is right in circumstances C_2. In X-land circumstances C_1 prevail, so A is right; and in Y-land circumstances C_2 prevail, so B is right. Perhaps this is all the relativism that ethical relativists will demand.

4. Can't there be, in rule-utilitarianism, a conflict of rules? Suppose you have to choose between breaking a promise and allowing a human life to be lost. . . . What would the rule-utilitarian say? Which rule are we to go by?

No rule-utilitarian would hold such a rule as "Never break a promise" or "Never take a human life." Following such rigid, unqualified rules would certainly not lead to the best consequences—for example, taking Hitler's life would have had better consequences than sparing him. Since such simple rules would never be incorporated into rule-utilitarian ethics to begin with, there would be no conflict between these rules. The rule-utilitarian's rule on taking human life would be of the form, "Do not take human life except in circumstances of types A, B, C . . ." and these circumstances would be those in which taking human life *would* have the best consequences. And the same with breaking promises. Thus, when the rules in question are fully spelled out, there would be no conflict.

In any event, if there were a conflict between rules, there would have to be a second-order rule to tell us which first-order rule to adopt in cases of conflict. Only with such a rule would our rule-utilitarian ethics be *complete*, i.e., made to cover every situation that might arise. But again such a second-order rule would seldom be simple. It would not say, "In cases of conflict between preserving a life and keeping a promise, always preserve the life." For there might always be kinds of cases in which this policy would not produce the best consequences: a president who has promised something to a whole nation or who has signed a treaty with other nations which depend on that treaty being kept and base their own national policies upon it, would not be well advised to say simply, "In cases of conflict, always break your word rather than lose one human life." In cases of this kind, keeping the promise would probably produce the best results, though the particular instance would have to be decided empirically. We would have to go through a detailed empirical examination to discover which rule, among all the rules we might adopt on the matter, would have the best consequences if adopted.

5. Well then, why not just make the whole thing simple and say, "Always keep your promises except when breaking them will produce the most good," "Always conserve human life except when taking it will produce the most good"? In other words, "In every case do what will have the best consequences"—why not make this the Rule of Rules? To do so is to have act-utilitarianism with us once again; but why not? It there anything more obvious in ethics than that we should always try to produce the most good possible?

"No," says the rule-utilitarian, "not if this rule means that we should always do the individual *act* that produces the most good possible. We must clearly distinguish rules from acts. 'Adopt the rule which will have the best consequences' is different from 'Do the act which will have the best consequences.' (When you say, 'Always do the most good,' this is ambiguous—it could mean either one.)" The rule-utilitarian, of course, recommends the former in preference to the latter; for if everyone were to do acts which (taken individually) had the best consequences, the result would *not* in every case be a policy having the best consequences. For example, my not voting but doing something else instead may produce better consequences than my voting (my voting may have no effect at all); your not voting will do the same; and so on for every individual, as long as most *other* people vote. But the results would be very bad, for if each individual adopted the policy of not voting, nobody would vote. In other words, the rule "Vote, except

119

in situations where not voting will do more good" is a rule which, if followed, would *not* produce the best consequences.

Another example: The rule "Don't kill except where killing will do the most good"—which the act-utilitarian would accept—is not, the rule-utilitarian would say, as good a rule to follow as "Don't kill except in self-defense . . ." (and other classes of acts which we discussed earlier). That is, the rule to prohibit killing except under special kinds of conditions specified in advance would do more good, if followed, than the rule simply to refrain except when not refraining will do more good. The former is better, not just because people will rationalize themselves into believing that what they want to do will produce the most good in a particular situation (though this is very important), but also because when there are certain standard classes of exceptions built into the rule, there will be a greater *predictability* of the results of such actions; the criminal will know what will happen if he is caught. If the law said, "Killing is prohibited except when it will do the most good," what could you expect? Every would-be killer would think it would do the most good in his specific situation. And would you, a potential victim, feel more secure or less secure, if such a law were enacted? Every criminal would think that he would be exonerated even if he were caught, and every victim (or would-be victim) would fear that this would be so. The effects of having such a rule, then, would be far worse than the effects of having a general rule prohibiting killing, with certain classes of qualifications built into the rule.

There is, then, it would seem, a considerable difference between act-utilitarianism and rule-utilitarianism.

A Defense of
Utilitarianism

R. M. HARE

R. M. Hare (b. 1919) is White's Professor of Moral Phi-
losophy at Corpus Christi College, Oxford University.
His books include *The Language of Morals, Freedom and
Reason*, and *Moral Theories*.

Hare distinguishes between two levels of moral thinking. In our everyday lives we operate at the "intuitive
level": we instinctively respond to situations without
carefully thinking them through. In more reflective
moments—the "critical level"—we carefully determine
which intuitions and loyalties are worth preserving and
fostering in people. Some intuitions—that parents
should prefer the interests of their children to those of
strangers, for example—are worth inculcating because
of their long-run utility. Others, such as patriotism, appear questionable. Deploying this distinction, Hare defends Utilitarianism from critics who claim it justifies
evil acts, such as punishing the innocent or killing derelicts in order to use their hearts and kidneys for trans-
plant surgery. Hare argues that such cases, which seem
to shake our intuitive commitments, are almost always
trumped up and artificial. In the very rare case in which
a utilitarian judgment would actually call for killing

A DEFENSE OF UTILITARIANISM   From *Moral Thinking* by R. M. Hare (Oxford University Press,
1981). © R. M. Hare 1981. Reprinted by permission of Oxford University Press.

someone, that act *would* be justified but it would then *not* be counterintuitive. Hare does not give an example of such a case, but presumably he would find it intuitively right to kill someone if it were sure that that was the only way to save many people from a horrible death. Intuitions are themselves subject to utilitarian calculus.

1. Suppose then that you are in a disputation with a utilitarian. Your object should be to enlist the sympathies of your audience on your side by showing that the utilitarian is committed to views which nearly everybody finds counterintuitive. What you have to do, therefore, is to find some moral opinion which nearly everybody will agree with, and bring utilitarianism into conflict with it. It is not necessary to choose for this purpose an opinion that can be defended by argument; any widely held prejudice will do. I have heard this kind of objection based on premises like 'Surely any theory is absurd which makes cruelty to animals as wicked as the same degree of cruelty to humans;' and no doubt in earlier centuries 'blacks' and 'whites' would have done as well. But obviously it is better if the opinion is a defensible one; the objection will then seem even more plausible.

Having selected your favoured received opinion, you can then proceed to bring utilitarianism into conflict with it in the following way. You find some example, rather simply described, in which, on an obvious interpretation of utilitarianism (and nearly all the versions of it can be made susceptible to this treatment, except for some versions of rule-utilitarianism which are highly implausible on other grounds) the utilitarian is committed to prescribing an act which almost everybody will agree is wrong. Give your case as much verisimilitude as you can. Professional opponents of utilitarianism are not always as careful as they should be about this. Sometimes they use extremely jejune examples, thinking the game to be a push-over, so that they need not take too much trouble with them. But it is better if the case is something which your audience can be got to believe really could happen. Thus you will seem to have established a knock-down counterinstance to the utilitarian theory; it will have been shown to require us to say some act is right when we all know it to be wrong.

2. Now suppose by contrast that you are on the opposite side in the disputation. . . .

. . . suppose that your opponent's case is the following: there are in a hospital two patients, one needing for survival a new heart and the other new kidneys; a down-and-out who is known to nobody and who happens to have the same tissue-type as both the patients strays in out of the cold. Ought they not to kill him, give his heart and kidneys to the patients, and thus save two lives at the expense of one? The utilitarian is supposed to have to say that they ought; the audience is supposed to say that they ought not, because it would be murder. Let us suppose that your opponent manages to get the audience to treat murder as a descriptive, not a secondarily evaluative, word . . . , and thus to call the statement that it would be murder a purely factual one, which can be established prior to any judgement that it would be wrong. I have simplified the case a little from the way it has sometimes been presented in the litera- ture . . . , because the complications will not affect the moves we shall be making.

On this example you have to mount a two-pronged attack. If we are to do intuitive thinking, the matter is fairly simple. It *is* murder, and *would* therefore be wrong. A utilitarian does not have to dissent from this verdict at the intuitive level. If he has been well brought up (and in particular if he has been brought up by a sound critical utilitarian thinker) he will have that intuition, and it is a very good thing, from the utilitarian point of view, that he will have it. For just think what would be the consequences of a moral education which contained no prohibition on murder!

Your opponent will now object that although on the utilitarian view it is a good thing for people to have these intuitions or feelings, it also follows from that view that they ought to overcome and act contrary to them in cases like this, in which, *ex hypothesi*, it is for the best to do so. Let us ask, then, whether the doctors in the hospital ought to do this if they are utilitarians. It will turn upon their estimate of the *probability* of hitting off the act which is for the best by so doing. The crucial words are, of course, '*ex hypothesi*;' for your opponent has constructed his example with the express purpose of making the murder the act which will have the best consequences. You must not allow him simply to *assume* that this is so; he has to convince the audience, not just that it really could be so in a real-life situation, but that it could be known to be so by the doctors with a high degree of probability. For utilitarianism, as a method of choosing the most rational action (the best bet for a utilitarian) in a moral dilemma of this sort, requires them to maximize the *expectation* of utility (i.e. preference-satisfaction); and since, if they get it wrong, the consequences will be pretty catastrophic, the doctors have to be very sure that they are not getting it wrong. There is perhaps no need to go into any technicalities of games-theory to establish this point, though a full account would need to contain a method of weighing combinations of probabilities with utilities against one another, by asking which combination one would prefer, after exposure to logic and the facts.

It is fairly obvious that this high degree of probability will not be forthcoming in many actual situations, if any at all. Have the doctors checked on the down-and-out's connexions or lack of them? (How? By consulting the police records, perhaps! But a colleague of my psychiatrist sister once wrote in his notes, about a dishevelled individual brought in off the streets very late at night by the police, 'Has delusion that he is a high-ranking civil servant,' and it turned out that he was in fact a *very* high-ranking civil servant.) Have they absolute confidence in the discretion and support of all the nurses, porters, mortuarists, etc., who will know what has happened? Add to this the extreme unlikelihood of there being no other way of saving these patients, if they can be saved at all, and it will be evident that your opponent is not going to get much help out of this example, once it is insisted that it has to be fleshed out and given verisimilitude.

But perhaps that was not his intention. Perhaps, that is to say, he all along intended the example to be a dummy. Is he not allowed, after a brief introduction of the example to give its general shape, to skip the details and simply *posit* that it is a case where murder would be for the best? The audience, which is probably prejudiced against utilitarians anyway, will have no difficulty in imagining that the details could be filled in in a way that would suit his case and damage yours. But you must not let him get away with this. If we are talking about intuitive thinking in a real-life sort of situation, the example needs to be a real-life sort of example.

. . .

Your opponent may say 'Are there not some cases occurring in real life, albeit rarely, in which murder is justified on utilitarian grounds?' To which you should reply that he has not produced any, but that if he really did find one, we should have to do some critical thinking on it because it would be clearly so unusual as to be beyond the range of our intuitions. If we then found that murder really was justified in that case, we still should not have shown that the rational moral agent would commit the murder; for he would be unlikely to have sufficient evidential grounds for saying that it was the right act. But, giving your opponent everything that he ask for, if he did actually have sufficient evidence (a very unlikely contingency), murder would *in that case* be justified; though even then the agent in question, if he had been well brought up, might not do it, because it would go so much against all his moral feelings, which in a good man are powerful. So, owing to being a good man, he might fail to do the right act. If he did bring himself to do it, it would haunt him for the rest of his life. But until your opponent produces actual cases, you should not let yourself be troubled overmuch with fictional ones. If the actual cases are produced, you will probably find that the critical discussion of them will leave you and the audience at one, provided that the discussion is serious.

3. We are now in a position to apply the same technique to some more genuine problems. Let us take first the objection commonly made to utilitarianism that it does not allow us to give any weight to the duties usually thought to exist towards particular persons, or to ties of affection and loyalty which bind us to them but not to mankind in general. . . . For example, it is usually held that we have special duties to our spouses and children, and ought to have greater affection and loyalty to them than to total strangers, and so seek their good more earnestly. Similar things are said about the relation between a doctor and his patient, or a teacher and his pupil. And similar things *used* to be universally, and are still quite widely, accepted about that between a citizen and his country. I have heard the same argued about the loyalty of a worker to his union.

These last two instances might make us pause before proceeding on the assumption that all commonly upheld loyalties can be used as a stick to beat utilitarians with. They show how palpable, and how dubious, is the appeal to intuition when people say that utilitarianism treats everybody's preferences as of equal weight (e.g. those of my children and other people's children), and therefore has to be rejected as giving no weight to these feelings of special affection which we all think it a good thing to encourage. We have first to be sure that, in a particular example, it *is* a good thing to encourage these feelings. Even family loyalties provide examples of extremely various intuitions. In some countries it is considered wrong if someone who has obtained a position of power does not use it to advance the interests of the members of his family; in others this is called nepotism and thought corrupt. And even in Britain there is dispute about whether it is right for a well endowed father to try to get the best possible education for his children by sending them to expensive schools which others cannot afford.

This should warn us that even where intuitions are all in agreement, they should not be taken for granted; it needs to be established by critical thought which of them ought, in our present circumstances, to be fostered. Anybody who asks himself whether, and in what sense, he ought to bring up his children to be patriotic will see the force of this question. So let us proceed as before and ask our anti-utilitarian objector what level of thinking he is talking about, intuitive or critical. In order to make it easy for him, let us allow him to choose an example in which nearly everybody will agree that the loyalty in question is a good thing. A mother, say, has a new-born child and her maternal feelings make her provide for this child, but they do not, or not to anything like the same degree, impel her to provide for other people's children. Ought a utilitarian to condemn this partiality?

At the intuitive level we all think that the mother is to be praised, in all normal circumstances (barring a few extreme radical advocates of communes, and Plato). Given our two-level structure, there is nothing in this that a utilitarian need object to. *If* the intuition is one that ought to be inculcated (and this cannot be determined without critical thinking), the most likely way of doing the right thing in normal circumstances will be to follow the intuition. If this were not so, then the intuition would not be the one which ought to be inculcated. If we ascend to the critical level and ask why it ought to be, the answer is fairly obvious. If mothers had the propensity to care equally for all the children in the world, it is unlikely that children would be as well provided for even as they are. The dilution of the responsibility would weaken it out of existence. Our traditional upbringing has taken account of this. And evidently Evolution (if we may personify her) has had the same idea; there are, we are told, a great many of these particular loyalties and affections which are genetically transmitted, and have no doubt favoured the survival of the genes which transmit them. . . .

4. The general lines of the utilitarian answer to this objection should by now be clear. *In so far* as the intuitions are desirable ones, they can be defended on utilitarian grounds by critical thinking, as having a high acceptance-utility; if they can be so defended, the best bet, even for an act-utilitarian, will be to cultivate them and follow them in all normal cases; if he cultivates them seriously, or has had them cultivated for him by those who brought him up, all the associated moral feelings will be present, but will provide no argument whatever against utilitarianism. Unlike intuitionism, it is actually able to *justify* the intuitions, where they can be justified.

Faced with this argument the anti-utilitarian will produce examples in which we would all have the intuitions, but in which, he asks us to suppose, the utilitarian would have to prescribe that we acted contrary to them. This would be because in the particular cases sufficient information is assumed to be available to show that the intuitively right act would not be for the best. To take a pasteboard example with which I was once confronted by Professor Bernard Williams on television: you are in an air crash and the aircraft catches fire, but you have managed to get out; in the burning plane are, among others, your son and a distinguished surgeon who could, if rescued, save many injured passengers' lives, to say nothing of those whose lives he would save in his subsequent career. You have time to rescue only one person.

It is hard to make Williams' example realistic. How do you know he is so distinguished a surgeon—perhaps he was only shooting a line when you struck up an acquaintance in the departure lounge? Has he got his tools with him, and can he do any more for the injured people than the first aid which the crew are trained to give (which probably prescribes keeping them warm and immobile and giving some common drugs which, we hope, they managed to extract from the aircraft)? How promising is your son's future (he can probably look forward to a greater span of it than the surgeon)?

However, setting aside all these minor points, we find that you have a very strong feeling that you ought to rescue your son and let the surgeon burn. But what does this show?

It would take a very hardened intuitionist to think that it shows that to rescue your son is your undoubted duty. You almost certainly will rescue your son. But that is because your have (rightly from the critical utilitarian point of view) been brought up to attach dominant importance to these family loyalties. Of course no upbringing takes into account such rare cases as this (they are not what those who influenced you were preparing you for, nor would evolution be affected by them). To be in an air crash of any sort is, fortunately, a statistically very rare experience; to be in one in which one has the opportunity to rescue anybody is rarer still; to be in one in which one can rescue precisely one person and no more is hardly to be expected. So you come to this unhappy experience entirely unprepared for it. Your intuitions were simply not designed to cope with it. However, you do have the strong moral feelings and will probably act on them in the split second which is all you have in which to decide. And who is to blame you? Probably in a situation of complete uncertainty and panic it is the rational thing to do. The fraudulence of the example consists in suggesting that you can at one and the same time be in this emergency situation, and do the leisured critical thinking which would be necessary in order to justify you in going against your intuitions.

Undoubtedly critics of utilitarianism will go on trying to produce examples which are both fleshed out and reasonably likely to occur, and also support their argument. I am prepared to bet, however, that the nearer they get to realism and specificity, and the further from playing trains—a sport which has had such a fascination for them—the more likely the audience is, on reflection, to accept the utilitarian solution. I am thinking of their examples in which trolleys hurtling down the line out of control have to be shunted into various alternative groups of unfortunate people. I have myself, when helping to build a railway, seen trolleys run out of control, and therefore find the unrealism of the examples very obvious. The point is that one has not time to think what to do, and so relies on one's immediate intuitive reactions; but these give no guide to what critical thinking would prescribe if there were time for it. But, personal experience aside, I have done quite a lot of work on serious practical problems in medicine, war, politics, urban planning and the like, and have never come across any actual example in which this kind of anti-utilitarian argument was in the least convincing.

Chapter

3

ETHICAL RELATIVISM

Morality as Custom

HERODOTUS

Herodotus (485–430 B.C.), a Greek, was the first Western historian. His work is the earliest Greek prose to
survive, and much of what we know about the ancient
world in and around Greece derives from him.

Herodotus is probably the first writer on morals to es-
pouse a version of what we today call Ethical Relativism.

If anyone, no matter who, were given the opportunity of choosing
from amongst all the nations in the world the set of beliefs which he
thought best, he would inevitably, after careful consideration of
their relative merits, choose that of his own country. Everyone
without exception believes his own native customs, and the religion
he was brought up in, to be the best; and that being so, it is unlikely
that anyone but a madman would mock at such things. There is
abundant evidence that this is the universal feeling about the ancient
customs of one's country. One might recall, in particular, an anec-
dote of Darius. When he was king of Persia, he summoned the
Greeks who happened to be present at his court, and asked them
what they would take to eat the dead bodies of their fathers. They
replied that they would not do it for any money in the world. Later,
in the presence of the Greeks, and through an interpreter, so that
they could understand what was said, he asked some Indians, of the
tribe called Callatiae, who do in fact eat their parents' dead bodies,
what they would take to burn them. They uttered a cry of horror

MORALITY AS CUSTOM From Herodotus' *The Histories*, translated by Aubrey de Selincourt (Penguin Classics, rev. ed. 1972), pp. 190–91. Copyright © the Estate of Aubrey de Selincourt, 1954.

and forbade him to mention such a dreadful thing. One can see by this what custom can do, and Pindar, in my opinion, was right when he called it 'king of all.'

A Defense of Ethical Relativism

RUTH BENEDICT

Ruth Benedict (1887–1948) was one of America's foremost anthropologists. Her *Patterns of Culture* (1935) is considered a classic of comparative anthropology.

Morality, says Benedict, is a convenient term for socially approved customs (mores). What one society approves may be disgraceful and unacceptable to another. Moral rules, like rules of etiquette or styles of dress, vary from society to society. Morality is culturally relative, and values are shaped by culture. As Benedict points out, trances are highly regarded in India, so in India many people have trances. Some ancient societies praised homosexual love, so for them homosexuality was a norm; where material possessions are highly valued, people amass property. "Most individuals are plastic to the moulding force of the society into which they are born."

Modern social anthropology has become more and more a study of the varieties and common elements of cultural environment and the consequences of these in human behavior. For such a study of diverse social orders primitive peoples fortunately provide a lab-

A DEFENSE OF ETHICAL RELATIVISM From "Anthropology and the Abnormal," by Ruth Benedict, in *The Journal of General Psychology*, 1934, vol. 10, pp. 59–82, a publication of the Helen Dwight Reid Educational Foundation.

133

oratory not yet entirely vitiated by the spread of a standardized worldwide civilization. Dyaks and Hopis, Fijians and Yakuts are significant for psychological and sociological study because only among these simpler peoples has there been sufficient isolation to give opportunity for the development of localized social forms. In the higher cultures the standardization of custom and belief over a couple of continents has given a false sense of the inevitability of the particular forms that have gained currency, and we need to turn to a wider survey in order to check the conclusions we hastily base upon this near-universality of familiar customs. Most of the simpler cultures did not gain the wide currency of the one which, out of our experience, we identify with human nature, but this was for various historical reasons, and certainly not for any that gives us as its carriers a monopoly of social good or of social sanity. Modern civilization, from this point of view, becomes not a necessary pinnacle of human achievement but one entry in a long series of possible adjustments.

These adjustments, whether they are in mannerisms like the ways of showing anger, or joy, or grief in any society, or in major human drives like those of sex, prove to be far more variable than experience in any one culture would suggest. In certain fields, such as that of religion or of formal marriage arrangements, these wide limits of variability are well known and can be fairly described. In others it is not yet possible to give a generalized account, but that does not absolve us of the task of indicating the significance of the work that has been done and of the problems that have arisen.

One of these problems relates to the customary modern normal-abnormal categories and our conclusions regarding them. In how far are such categories culturally determined, or in how far can we with assurance regard them as absolute? In how far can we regard inability to function socially as diagnostic of abnormality, or in how far is it necessary to regard this as a function of the culture?

As a matter of fact, one of the most striking facts that emerge from a study of widely varying cultures is the ease with which our abnormals function in other cultures. It does not matter what kind of "abnormality" we choose for illustration, those which indicate extreme instability, or those which are more in the nature of character traits like sadism or delusions of grandeur or of persecution, there are well-described cultures in which these abnormals function at ease and with honor, and apparently without danger or difficulty to the society.

The most notorious of these is trance and catalepsy. Even a very mild mystic is aberrant in our culture. But most peoples have regarded even extreme psychic manifestations not only as normal and desirable, but even as characteristic of highly valued and gifted individuals. This was true even in our own cultural background in that period when Catholicism made the ecstatic experience the mark of sainthood. It is hard for us, born and brought up in a culture that makes no use of the experience, to realize how important a role it may play and how many individuals are capable of it, once it has been given an honorable place in any society. . . .

Cataleptic and trance phenomena are, of course, only one illustration of the fact that those whom we regard as abnormals may function adequately in other cultures. Many of our culturally discarded traits are selected for elaboration in different societies. Homosexuality is an excellent example, for in this case our attention is not constantly diverted, as in the consideration of trance, to the interruption of routine activity which it implies. Homosexuality poses the problem very simply. A tendency toward this trait in our culture exposes an individual to all the conflicts to which all aberrants are always exposed, and we tend to identify the consequences of this conflict with homosexuality. But these consequences are obviously local and cultural. Homosexuals in many societies are not incompetent, but they may be such if the culture asks adjustments of them that would strain any man's vitality. Wherever homosexuality has been given an honorable place in any society, those to whom it is congenial have filled adequately the honorable roles society assigns to them. Plato's *Republic* is, of course, the most convincing statement of such a reading of homosexuality. It is presented as one of the major means to the good life, and it was generally so regarded in Greece at that time.

The cultural attitude toward homosexuals has not always been on such a high ethical plane, but it has been very varied. Among many American Indian tribes there exists the institution of the berdache, as the French called them. These men-women were men who at puberty or thereafter took the dress and the occupations of women. Sometimes they married other men and lived with them. Sometimes they were men with no inversion, persons of weak sexual endowment who chose this role to avoid the jeers of the women. The berdaches were never regarded as of first-rate supernatural power, as similar men-women were in Siberia, but rather as leaders in women's occupations, good healers in certain diseases, or, among certain tribes, as the genial organizers of social affairs. In any case, they were socially placed. They were not left exposed to the conflicts that visit the deviant who is excluded from participation in the recognized patterns of his society.

The most spectacular illustrations of the extent to which normality may be culturally defined are those cultures where an abnormality of our culture is the cornerstone of their social structure. It is not possible to do justice to these possibilities in a short discussion. A recent study of an island of northwest Melanesia by Fortune describes a society built upon traits which we regard as beyond the border of paranoia. In this tribe the exogamic groups look upon each other as prime manipulators of black magic, so that one marries always into an enemy group which remains for life one's deadly and unappeasable foes. They look upon a good garden crop as a confession of theft, for everyone is engaged in making magic to induce into his garden the productiveness of his neighbors'; therefore no secrecy in the island is so rigidly insisted upon as the secrecy of a man's harvesting of his yams. Their polite phrase at the acceptance of a gift is, "And if you now poison me, how shall I repay you this present?" Their preoccupation with poisoning is constant; no woman ever leaves her cooking pot for a moment untended. Even the great affinal economic exchanges that are characteristic of this Melanesian culture area are quite altered in Dobu since they are incompatible with this fear and distrust that pervades the culture. They go farther and people the whole world outside their own quarters with such malignant spirits that all-night feasts and ceremonials simply do not occur here. They have even rigorous religiously enforced customs that forbid the sharing of seed even in one family group. Anyone else's food is deadly poison to you, so that communality of stores is out of the question. For some months before harvest the whole society is on the verge of starvation, but if one falls to the temptation and eats up one's seed yams, one is an outcast and a beachcomber for life. There is no coming back. It involves, as a matter of course, divorce and the breaking of all social ties.

Now in this society where no one may work with another and no one may share with another, Fortune describes the individual who was regarded by all his fellows as crazy. He was not one of those who periodically ran amok and, beside himself and frothing at the mouth, fell with a knife upon anyone he could reach. Such behavior they did not regard as putting anyone outside the pale. They did not even put the individuals who were known to be liable to these attacks under any kind of control. They merely fled when they saw the attack coming on and kept out of the way. "He would be all right tomorrow." But there was one man of sunny, kindly disposition who liked work and liked to be helpful. The compulsion was too strong for him to repress it in favor of the opposite tendencies of his culture. Men and women never spoke of him without laughing; he was silly and simple and definitely crazy. Nevertheless, to the ethnologist used to a culture that has, in Christianity, made his type the model of all virtue, he seemed a pleasant fellow. . . .

. . . Among the Kwakiutl it did not matter whether a relative had died in bed of disease, or by the hand of an enemy, in either case death was an affront to be wiped out by the death of another person. The fact that one had been caused to mourn was proof that one had been put upon. A chief's sister and her daughter had gone up to Victoria, and either because they drank bad whiskey or because their boat capsized they never came back. The chief called together his warriors, "Now I ask you, tribes, who shall wail? Shall I do it or shall another?" The spokesman answered, of course, "Not you, Chief. Let some other of the tribes." Immediately they set up the war pole to announce their intention of wiping out the injury, and gathered a war party. They set out, and found seven men and two children asleep and killed them. "Then they felt good when they arrived at Sebaa in the evening."

The point which is of interest to us is that in our society those who on that occasion would feel good when they arrived at Sebaa that evening would be the definitely abnormal. There would be some, even in our society, but it is not a recognized and approved mood under the circumstances. On the Northwest Coast those are favored and fortunate to whom that mood under those circumstances is congenial, and those to whom it is repugnant are unlucky. This latter minority can register in their own culture only by doing violence to their congenial responses and acquiring others that are difficult for them. The person, for instance, who, like a Plains Indian whose wife has been taken from him, is too proud to fight, can deal with the Northwest Coast civilization only by ignoring its strongest bents. If he cannot achieve it, he is the deviant in that culture, their instance of abnormality.

This head-hunting that takes place on the Northwest Coast after a death is no matter of blood revenge or of organized vengeance. There is no effort to tie up the subsequent killing with any responsibility on the part of the victim for the death of the person who is being mourned. A chief whose son has died goes visiting wherever his fancy dictates, and he says to his host, "My prince has died today, and you go with him." Then he kills him. In this, according to their interpretation, he acts nobly because he has not been downed. He has thrust back in return. The whole procedure is meaningless without the fundamental paranoid reading of bereavement. Death, like all the other untoward accidents of existence, confounds man's pride and can only be handled in the category of insults.

Behavior honored upon the Northwest Coast is one which is recognized as abnormal in our civilization, and yet it is sufficiently close to the attitudes of our own culture to be intelligible to us and to have a definite vocabulary with which we may discuss it. The megalomaniac paranoid trend is a definite danger in our society. It is encouraged by some of our major preoccupations, and it confronts us with a choice of two possible attitudes. One is to brand it as abnormal and reprehensible, and is the attitude we have chosen in our civilization. The other is to make it an essential attribute of ideal man, and this is the solution in the culture of the Northwest Coast.

These illustrations, which it has been possible to indicate only in the briefest manner, force upon us the fact that normality is culturally defined. An adult shaped to the drives and standards of either of these cultures, if he were transported into our civilization, would fall into our categories of abnormality. He would be faced with the psychic dilemmas of the socially unavailable. In his own culture, however, he is the pillar of society, the end result of socially inculcated mores, and the problem of personal instability in his case simply does not arise.

No one civilization can possibly utilize in its mores the whole potential range of human behavior. Just as there are great numbers of possible phonetic articulations, and the possibility of language depends on a selection and standardization of a few of these in order that speech communication may be possible at all, so the possibility of organized behavior of every sort, from the fashions of local dress and houses to the dicta of a people's ethics and religion, depends upon a similar selection among the possible behavior traits. In the field of recognized economic obligations or sex tabus this selection is as nonrational and subconscious a process as it is in the field of phonetics. It is a process which goes on in the group for long periods of time and is historically conditioned by innumerable accidents of isolation or of contact of peoples. In any comprehensive study of psychology, the selection that different cultures have made in the course of history within the great circumference of potential behavior is of great significance.

Every society, beginning with some slight inclination in one direction or another, carries its preference farther and farther, integrating itself more and more completely upon its chosen basis, and discarding those types of behavior that are uncongenial. Most of those organizations of personality that seem to us most uncontrovertibly abnormal have been used by different civilizations in the very foundations of their institutional life. Conversely the most valued traits of our normal individuals have been looked on in differently organized cultures as aberrant. Normality, in short, within a very wide range, is culturally defined. It is primarily a term for the socially elaborated segment of human behavior in any culture; and abnormality, a term for the segment that that particular civilization does not use. The very eyes with which we see the problem are conditioned by the long traditional habits of our own society.

It is a point that has been made more often in relation to ethics than in relation to psychiatry. We do not any longer make the mistake of deriving the morality of our locality and decade directly from the inevitable constitution of human nature. We do not elevate it to the dignity of a first principle. We recognize that morality differs in every society, and is a convenient term for socially approved habits. Mankind has always preferred to say, "It is a morally good," rather than "It is habitual," and the fact of this preference is matter enough for a critical science of ethics. But historically the two phrases are synonymous.

139

The concept of the normal is properly a variant of the concept of the good. It is that which society has approved. A normal action is one which falls well within the limits of expected behavior for a particular society. Its variability among different peoples is essentially a function of the variability of the behavior patterns that different societies have created for themselves, and can never be wholly divorced from a consideration of culturally institutionalized types of behavior.

Each culture is a more or less elaborate working-out of the potentialities of the segment it has chosen. In so far as a civilization is well integrated and consistent within itself, it will tend to carry farther and farther, according to its nature, its initial impulse toward a particular type of action, and from the point of view of any other culture those elaborations will include more and more extreme and aberrant traits.

Each of these traits, in proportion as it reinforces the chosen behavior patterns of that culture, is for that culture normal. Those individuals to whom it is congenial either congenitally, or as the result of childhood sets, are accorded prestige in that culture, and are not visited with the social contempt or disapproval which their traits would call down upon them in a society that was differently organized. On the other hand, those individuals whose characteristics are not congenial to the selected type of human behavior in that community are the deviants, no matter how valued their personality traits may be in a contrasted civilization.

The Dobuan who is not easily susceptible to fear of treachery, who enjoys work and likes to be helpful, is their neurotic and regarded as silly. On the Northwest Coast the person who finds it difficult to read life in terms of an insult contest will be the person upon whom fall all the difficulties of the culturally unprovided for. The person who does not find it easy to humiliate a neighbor, nor to see humiliation in his own experience, who is genial and loving, may, of course, find some unstandardized way of achieving satisfactions in his society, but not in the major patterned responses that his culture requires of him. If he is born to play an important role in a family with many hereditary privileges, he can succeed only by doing violence to his whole personality. If he does not succeed, he has betrayed his culture; that is, he is abnormal.

I have spoken of individuals as having sets toward certain types of behavior, and of these sets as running sometimes counter to the types of behavior which are institutionalized in the culture to which they belong. From all that we know of contrasting cultures it seems clear that differences of temperament occur in every society. The matter has never been made the subject of investigation, but from the available material it would appear that these temperament types are very likely of universal recurrence. That is, there is an ascertainable range of human behavior that is found wherever a sufficiently large series of individuals is observed. But the proportion in which behavior types stand to one another in different societies is not universal. The vast majority of individuals in any group are shaped to the fashion of that culture. In other words, most individuals are plastic to the moulding force of the society into which they are born. In a society that values trance, as in India, they will have supernormal experience. In a society that institutionalizes homosexuality, they will be homosexual. In a society that sets the gathering of possessions as the chief human objective, they will amass property. The deviants, whatever the type of behavior the culture has institutionalized, will remain few in number, and there seems no more difficulty in moulding the vast malleable majority to the "normality" of what we consider an aberrant trait, such as delusions of reference, than to the normality of such accepted behavior patterns as acquisitiveness. The small proportion of the number of the deviants in any culture is not a function of the sure instinct with which that society has built itself upon the fundamental sanities, but of the universal fact that, happily, the majority of mankind quite readily take any shape that is presented to them. . . .

Ethical Relativism:
A Critique

W. T. STACE

Walter Terence Stace (1886–1967) was a professor of philosophy at Princeton University. He is the author of a
number of highly acclaimed books in the philosophy of
religion, metaphysics, and ethics.

The ethical relativist claims that there are no objective
moral standards: right and wrong vary from culture to
culture. Stace criticizes this view and defends its opposite: ethical absolutism. According to ethical absolutism,
all people everywhere are accountable to certain universal moral standards. The fact that not all societies are
aware of these standards just shows that such a thing as
moral ignorance exists. Stace argues that ethical relativism makes it impossible to compare societies as morally
better or worse. Stace also points out the difficulties of
determining what constitutes a cultural group. (Does the
American nation constitute a group having a single
moral standard?) Rejecting all religious solutions, Stace
acknowledges the difficulties facing the absolutist in providing the basis for a universal morality. But he is hope-

ETHICAL RELATIVISM: A CRITIQUE   From *The Concept of Morals* by Walter T. Stace. Copyright 1937
by Macmillan Publishing Co., Inc., renewed 1965 by Walter T. Stace. Reprinted with permission
of Macmillan Publishing Company.

ful that philosophers will work it out. Meanwhile, he advises that we reject the tempting but incoherent and demoralizing doctrine of ethical relativism.

I

Any ethical position which denies that there is a single moral standard which is equally applicable to all men at all times may fairly be called a species of ethical relativity. There is not, the relativist asserts, merely one moral law, one code, one standard. There are many moral laws, codes, standards. What morality ordains in one place or age may be quite different from what morality ordains in another place or age. The moral code of Chinamen is quite different from that of Europeans, that of African savages quite different from both. Any morality, therefore, is relative to the age, the place, and the circumstances in which it is found. It is in no sense absolute.

This does not mean merely—as one might at first sight be inclined to suppose—that the very same kind of action which is *thought* right in one country and period may be *thought* wrong in another. This would be a mere platitude, the truth of which everyone would have to admit. Even the absolutist would admit this— would even wish to emphasize it—since he is well aware that different people have different sets of moral ideas, and his whole point is that some of these sets of ideas are false. What the relativist means to assert is, not this platitude, but that the very same kind of action which *is* right in one country and period may *be* wrong in another. And this, far from being a platitude, is a very startling assertion.

It is very important to grasp thoroughly the difference between the two ideas. For there is reason to think that many minds tend to find ethical relativity attractive because they fail to keep them clearly apart. It is so very obvious that moral ideas differ from country to country and from age to age. And it is so very easy, if you are mentally lazy, to suppose that to say this means the same as to say that no universal moral standard exists—or in other words that it implies ethical relativity. We fail to see that the word "standard" is used in two different senses. It is perfectly true that, in one sense, there are many variable moral standards. We speak of judging a man by the standard of his time. And this implies that different times have different standards. And this, of course, is quite true. But when the word "standard" is used in this sense it means simply the set of moral ideas current during the period in question. It means what people *think* right, whether as a matter of fact it *is* right or not. On the other hand when the absolutist asserts that there exists a single universal moral "standard," he is not using the word in this sense at all. He means by "standard" what *is* right as distinct from what people merely think right. His point is that although what people think right varies in different countries and periods, yet what actually is right is everywhere and always the same. And it follows that when the ethical relativist disputes the position of the absolutist and denies that any universal moral standard exists, he too means by "standard" what actually is right. But it is exceedingly easy, if we are not careful, to slip loosely from using the word in the first sense to using it in the second sense, and to suppose that the variability of moral beliefs is the same thing as the variability of what really is moral. And unless we keep the two senses of the word "standard" distinct, we are likely to think the creed of ethical relativity much more plausible than it actually is.

The genuine relativist, then, does not merely mean that Chinamen may think right what Frenchmen think wrong. He means that what *is* wrong for the Frenchman may *be* right for the Chinaman. And if one inquires how, in those circumstances, one is to know what actually is right in China or in France, the answer comes quite glibly. What is right in China is the same as what people think right in China; and what is right in France is the same as what people think right in France. So that if you want to know what is moral in any particular country or age, all you have to do is to ascertain what are the moral ideas current in that age or country. Those ideas are, *for that age or country,* right. Thus what is morally right is identified with what is thought to be morally right, and the distinction which we made above between these two is simply denied. To put the same thing in another way, it is denied that there can be or ought to be any distinction between the two senses of the word "standard." There is only one kind of standard of right and wrong, namely, the moral ideas current in any particular age or country.

Moral right *means* what people think morally right. It has no other meaning. What Frenchmen think right is, therefore, right *for Frenchmen.* And evidently one must conclude—though I am not aware that relativists are anxious to draw one's attention to such unsavory but yet absolutely necessary conclusions from their creed—that cannibalism is right for people who believe in it, that human sacrifice is right for those races which practice it, and that burning widows alive was right for Hindus until the British stepped in and compelled the Hindus to behave immorally by allowing their widows to remain alive.

When it is said that, according to the ethical relativist, what is thought right in any social group is right for that group, one must be careful not to misinterpret this. The relativist does not, of course, mean that there actually is an objective moral standard in France and a different objective standard in England, and that French and British opinions respectively give us correct information about these different standards. His point is rather that there are not objectively true moral standards at all. There is no single universal objective standard. Nor are there a variety of local objective standards. All standards are subjective. People's subjective feelings about morality are the only standards which exist.

To sum up: The ethical relativist consistently denies, it would seem, whatever the ethical absolutist asserts. For the absolutist there is a single universal moral standard. For the relativist there is no such standard. There are only local, ephemeral, and variable standards. For the absolutist there are two senses of the word "standard." Standards in the sense of sets of current moral ideas are relative and changeable. But the standard in the sense of what is actually morally right is absolute and unchanging. For the relativist no such distinction can be made. There is only one meaning of the word standard, namely, that which refers to local and variable sets of moral ideas. Or if it is insisted that the word must be allowed two meanings, then the relativist will say that there is at any rate no actual example of a standard in the absolute sense, and that the word as thus used is an empty name to which nothing in reality corresponds; so that the distinction between the two meanings becomes empty and useless. Finally—though this is merely saying the same thing in another way—the absolutist makes a distinction between what actually is right and what is thought right. The relativist rejects this distinction and identifies what is moral with what is thought moral by certain human beings or groups of human beings. . . .

II

I shall now proceed to consider, first, the main arguments which can be urged in favor of ethical relativity; and secondly, the arguments which can be urged against it. . . . The first [in favor] is that which relies upon the actual varieties of moral "standards" found in the world. It was easy enough to believe in a single absolute morality in older times when there was no anthropology, when all humanity was divided clearly into two groups, Christian peoples and the "heathen." Christian peoples knew and possessed the one true morality. The rest were savages whose moral ideas could be ignored. But all this is changed. Greater knowledge has brought greater tolerance. We can no longer exalt our own morality as alone true, while dismissing all other moralities as false or inferior. The investigations of anthropologists have shown that there exists side by side in the world a bewildering variety of moral codes. On this topic endless volumes have been written, masses of evidence piled up. Anthropologists have ransacked the Melanesian Islands, the jungles of New Guinea, the steppes of Siberia, the deserts of Australia, the forests of central Africa, and have brought back with them countless examples of weird, extravagant, and fantastic "moral" customs with which to confound us. We learn that all kinds of horrible practices are, in this, that, or the other place, regarded as essential to virtue. We find that there is nothing, or next to nothing, which has always and everywhere been regarded as morally good by all men. Where, then, is our universal morality? Can we, in face of all this evidence, deny that it is nothing but an empty dream?

This argument, taken by itself, is a very weak one. It relies upon a single set of facts—the variable moral customs of the world. But this variability of moral ideas is admitted by both parties to the dispute, and is capable of ready explanation upon the hypothesis of either party. The relativist says that the facts are to be explained by the nonexistence of any absolute moral standard. The absolutist says that they are to be explained by human ignorance of what the absolute moral standard is. And he can truly point out that men have differed widely in their opinions about all manner of topics—including the subject-matters of the physical sciences—just as much as they differ about morals. And if the various different opinions which men have held about the shape of the earth do not prove that it has no one real shape, neither do the various opinions which they have held about morality prove that there is no one true morality.

Thus the facts can be explained equally plausibly on either hypothesis. There is nothing in the facts themselves which compels us to prefer the relativistic hypothesis to that of the absolutist. And therefore the argument fails to prove the relativist conclusion. If that conclusion is to be established, it must be by means of other considerations.

This is the essential point. But I will add some supplementary remarks. The work of the anthropologists, upon which ethical relativists seem to rely so heavily, has as a matter of fact added absolutely nothing *in principle* to what has always been known about the variability of moral ideas. Educated people have known all along that the Greeks tolerated sodomy, which in modern times has been regarded in some countries as an abominable crime; that the Hindus thought it a sacred duty to burn their widows; that trickery, now thought despicable, was once believed to be a virtue; that terrible torture was thought by our own ancestors only a few centuries ago to be a justifiable weapon of justice; that it was only yesterday that western peoples came to believe that slavery is immoral. Even the ancients knew very well that moral customs and ideas vary—witness the writings of Herodotus. Thus the principle of the variability of moral ideas was well understood long before modern anthropology was ever heard of. Anthropology has added nothing to the knowledge of this principle except a mass of new and extreme examples of it drawn from very remote sources. But to multiply examples of a principle already well known and universally admitted adds nothing to the argument which is built upon that principle. The discoveries of the anthropologists have no doubt been of the highest importance in their own sphere. But in any considered opinion they have thrown no new light upon the special problems of the moral philosopher.

Although the multiplication of examples has no logical bearing on the argument, it does have an immense *psychological* effect upon people's minds. These masses of anthropological learning are impressive. They are propounded in the sacred name of "science." If they are quoted in support of ethical relativity—as they often are—people *think* that they must prove something important. They bewilder and over-awe the simple-minded, batter down their

147

resistance, make them ready to receive humbly the doctrine of ethical relativity from those who have acquired a reputation by their immense learning and their claims to be "scientific." Perhaps this is why so much ado is made by ethical relativists regarding the anthropological evidence. But we must refuse to be impressed. We must discount all this mass of evidence about the extraordinary moral customs of remote peoples. Once we have admitted—as everyone who is instructed must have admitted these last two thousand years without any anthropology at all—the principle that moral ideas vary, all this new evidence adds nothing to the argument. And the argument itself proves nothing for the reasons already given. . . .

The second argument in favor of ethical relativity . . . does not suffer from the disadvantage that it is dependent upon the acceptance of any particular philosophy such as radical empiricism. It makes its appeal to considerations of a quite general character. It consists in alleging that no one has ever been able to discover upon what foundation an absolute morality could rest, or from what source a universally binding moral code could derive its authority.

If, for example, it is an absolute and unalterable moral rule that all men ought to be unselfish, from whence does this *command* issue? For a command it certainly is, phrase it how you please. There is no difference in meaning between the sentence "You ought to be unselfish" and the sentence "Be unselfish." Now a command implies a commander. An obligation implies some authority which obliges. Who is this commander, what this authority? Thus the vastly difficult question is raised of *the basis of moral obligation*. Now the argument of the relativist would be that it is impossible to find any basis for a universally binding moral law; but that it is quite easy to discover a basis for morality if moral codes are admitted to be variable, ephemeral, and relative to time, place, and circumstance.

In this paper I am assuming that it is no longer possible to solve this difficulty by saying naively that the universal moral law is based upon the uniform commands of God to all men. There will be many, no doubt, who will dispute this. But I am not writing for them. I am writing for those who feel the necessity of finding for morality a basis independent of particular religious dogmas. And I shall therefore make no attempt to argue the matter.

The problem which the absolutist has to face, then, is this. The religious basis of the one absolute morality having disappeared, can there be found for it any other, any secular, basis? If not, then it would seem that we cannot any longer believe in absolutism. We shall have to fall back upon belief in a variety of perhaps mutually inconsistent moral codes operating over restricted areas and limited periods. No one of these will be better, or more true, than any other. Each will be good and true for those living in those areas and periods. We shall have to fall back, in a word, on ethical relativity.

For there is no great difficulty in discovering the foundations of morality, or rather of moralities, if we adopt the relativistic hypothesis. Even if we cannot be quite certain *precisely* what these foundations are—and relativists themselves are not entirely agreed about them—we can at least see in a general way the *sort* of foundations they must have. We can see that the question on this basis is not in principle impossible of answer—although the details may be obscure; while, if we adopt the absolutist hypothesis—so the argument runs—no kind of answer is conceivable at all. . . .

This argument is undoubtedly very strong. It *is* absolutely essential to solve the problem of the basis of moral obligation if we are to believe in any kind of moral standards other than those provided by mere custom or by irrational emotions. It is idle to talk about a univeral morality unless we can point to the source of its authority—or at least to do so is to indulge in a faith which is without rational ground. To cherish a blind faith in morality may be, for the average man whose business is primarily to live right and not to theorize, sufficient. Perhaps it is his wisest course. But it will not do for the philosopher. His function, or at least one of his functions, is precisely to discover the rational grounds of our everyday beliefs—if they have any. Philosophically and intellectually, then, we cannot accept belief in a universally binding morality unless we can discover upon what foundation its obligatory character rests.

But in spite of the strength of the argument thus posed in favor of ethical relativity, it is not impregnable. For it leaves open one loophole. It is always possible that some theory, not yet examined, may provide a basis for a universal moral obligation. The argument rests upon the [universal] negative proposition that *there is no theory which can provide a basis for a universal morality*. But it is notoriously difficult to prove a negative. How can you prove that there are no green swans? All you can show is that none have been found so far. And then it is always possible that one will be found tomorrow. . . .

III

It is time that we turn our attention from the case in favor of ethical relativity to the case against it. Now the case against it consists, to a very large extent, in urging that, if taken seriously and pressed to its logical conclusion, ethical relativity can only end in destroying the conception of morality altogether, in undermining its practical efficacy, in rendering meaningless many almost universally accepted truths about human affairs, in robbing human beings of any incentive to strive for a better world, in taking the life-blood out of every ideal and every aspiration which has ever ennobled the life of man. . . .

First of all, then, ethical relativity, in asserting that the moral standards of particular social groups are the only standards which exist, renders meaningless all propositions which attempt to compare these standards with one another in respect of their moral worth. And this is a very serious matter indeed. We are accustomed to think that the moral ideas of one nation or social group may be "higher" or "lower" than those of another. We believe, for example, that Christian ethical ideals are nobler than those of the savage races of central Africa. Probably most of us would think that the Chinese moral standards are higher than those of the inhabitants of New Guinea. In short we habitually compare one civilization with another and judge the sets of ethical ideas to be found in them to be some better, some worse. The fact that such judgments are very difficult to make with any justice, and that they are frequently made on very superficial and prejudiced grounds, has no bearing on the question now at issue. The question is whether such judgments have any *meaning*. We habitually assume that they have.

But on the basis of ethical relativity they can have none whatever. For the relativist must hold that there is no *common* standard which can be applied to the various civilizations judged. Any such comparison of moral standards implies the existence of some superior standard which is applicable to both. And the existence of any such standard is precisely what the relativist denies. According to him the Christian standard is applicable only to Christians, the

Chinese standard only to Chinese, the New Guinea standard only to the inhabitants of New Guinea.

What is true of comparisons between the moral standards of different races will also be true of comparisons between those of different ages. It is not unusual to ask such questions as whether the standard of our own day is superior to that which existed among our ancestors five hundred years ago. And when we remember that our ancestors employed slaves, practiced barbaric physical tortures, and burned people alive, we may be inclined to think that it is. At any rate we assume that the question is one which has meaning and is capable of rational discussion. But if the ethical relativist is right, whatever we assert on this subject must be totally meaningless. For here again there is no common standard which could form the basis of any such judgments.

This in its turn implies that the whole notion of moral *progress* is a sheer delusion. Progress means an advance from lower to higher, from worse to better. But on the basis of ethical relativity it has no meaning to say that the standards of this age are better (or worse) than those of a previous age. For there is no common standard by which both can be measured. Thus it is nonsense to say that the morality of the New Testament is higher than that of the Old. And Jesus Christ, if he imagined that he was introducing into the world a higher ethical standard than existed before his time, was merely deluded. . . .

I come now to a second point. Up to the present I have allowed it to be taken tacitly for granted that, though judgments comparing different races and ages in respect of the worth of their moral codes are impossible for the ethical relativist, yet judgments of comparison between individuals living within the same social group would be quite possible. For individuals living within the same social group would presumably be subject to the same moral code, that of their group, and this would therefore constitute, as between these individuals, a common standard by which they could both be measured. We have not here, as we had in the other case, the difficulty of the absence of any common standard of comparison. It should therefore be possible for the ethical relativist to say quite meaningfully that President Lincoln was a better man than some criminal or moral imbecile of his own time and country, or that Jesus was a better man than Judas Iscariot.

But is even this minimum of moral judgment really possible on relativist grounds? It seems to me that it is not. For when once the whole of humanity is abandoned as the area covered by a single moral standard, what smaller areas are to be adopted as the *loci* of different standards? Where are we to draw the lines of demarcation? We can split up humanity, perhaps—though the procedure will be very arbitrary—into races, races into nations, nations into tribes, tribes into families, families into individuals. Where are we going to draw the *moral* boundaries? Does the *locus* of a particular moral standard reside in a race, a nation, a tribe, a family, or an individual? Perhaps the blessed phrase "social group" will be dragged in to save the situation. Each such group, we shall be told, has its own moral code which is, for it, right. But what *is* a "group"? Can any one define it or give its boundaries? This is the seat of that ambiguity in the theory of ethical relativity to which reference was made on an earlier page.

The difficulty is not, as might be thought, merely an academic difficulty of logical definition. If that were all, I should not press the point. But the ambiguity has practical consequences which are disastrous for morality. No one is likely to say that moral codes are confined within the arbitrary limits of the geographical divisions of countries. Nor are the notions of race, nation, or political state likely to help us. To bring out the essentially practical character of the difficulty let us put it in the form of concrete questions. Does the American nation constitute a "group" having a single moral standard? Or does the standard of what I ought to do change continuously as I cross the continent in a railway train? Do different States of the Union have different moral codes? Perhaps every town and village has its own peculiar standard. This may at first sight seem reasonable enough. "In Rome do as Rome does" may seem as good a rule in morals as it is in etiquette. But can we stop there? Within the village are numerous cliques each having its own set of ideas. Why should not each of these claim to be bound only by its own special and peculiar moral standards? And if it comes to that, why should not the gangsters of Chicago claim to constitute a group having its own morality, so that its murders and debaucheries must be viewed as "right" by the only standard which can legitimately be applied to it? And if it be answered that the nation will not tolerate this, that may be so. But this is to put the foundation of right simply in the superior force of the majority. In that case whoever is stronger will be right, however monstrous his ideas and actions. And if we cannot deny to any set of people the right to have its own morality, is it not clear that, in the end, we cannot even deny this right to the individual? Every individual man and woman can put up, on this view, an irrefutable claim to be judged by no standard except his or her own.

If these arguments are valid, the ethical relativist cannot really maintain that there is anywhere to be found a moral standard binding upon anybody against his will. And he cannot maintain that, even within the social group, there is a common standard as between individuals. And if that is so, then even judgments to the effect that one man is morally better than another become meaningless. All moral valuation thus vanishes. There is nothing to prevent each man from being a rule unto himself. The result will be moral chaos and the collapse of all effective standards. . . .

But even if we assume that the difficulty about defining moral groups has been surmounted, a further difficulty presents itself. Suppose that we have now definitely decided what are the exact boundaries of the social group within which a moral standard is to be operative. And we will assume—as is invariably done by relativists themselves—that this group is to be some actually existing social community such as a tribe or nation. How are we to know, even then, what actually is the moral standard within that group? How is anyone to know? How is even a member of the group to know? For there are certain to be within the group—at least this will be true among advanced peoples—wide differences of opinion as to what is right, what wrong. Whose opinion, then, is to be taken as representing *the* moral standard of the group? Either we must take the opinion of the majority within the group, or the opinion of some minority. If we rely upon the ideas of the majority, the results will be disastrous. Wherever there is found among a people a small band of select spirits, or perhaps one man, working for the establishment of higher and nobler ideas than those commonly accepted by the group, we shall be compelled to hold that, for that people at that time, the majority are right, and that the reformers are wrong and are preaching what is immoral. We shall have to maintain, for example, that Jesus was preaching immoral doctrines to the Jews. Moral goodness will have to be equated always with the mediocre and sometimes with the definitely base and ignoble. If on the other hand we said that the moral standard of the group is to be identified with the moral opinions of some minority, then what minority is this to be? We cannot answer that it is to be the minority composed of the best and the most enlightened individuals of the group. This would involve us in a palpably vicious circle. For by what standard are these individuals to be judged the best and the most enlightened? There is no principle by which we could select the right minority. And therefore we should have to consider every minority as good as every other. And this means that we should have no logical right whatever to resist the claim of the gangsters of Chicago—if such a claim were made— that their practices represent the highest standards of American morality. It means in the end that every individual is to be bound by no standard save his own.

The ethical relativists are great empiricists. *What* is the actual moral standard of any group can only be discovered, they tell us, by an examination on the ground of the moral opinions and customs of that group. But will they tell us how they propose to decide, when they get to the ground, which of the many moral opinions they are sure to find there is *the* right one in that group? To some extent they will be able to do this for the Melanesian Islanders—from whom apparently all lessons in the nature of morality are in future to be taken. But it is certain that they cannot do it for advanced peoples whose members have learned to think for themselves and to entertain among themselves a wide variety of opinions. They cannot do it unless they accept the calamitous view that the ethical opinion of the majority is always right. We are left therefore once more with the conclusion that, even within a particular social group, anybody's moral opinion is as good as anybody's else's, and that every man is entitled to be judged by his own standards.

Finally, not only is ethical relativity disastrous in its consequences for moral theory. It cannot be doubted that it must tend to be equally disastrous in its impact upon practical conduct. If men come really to believe that one moral standard is as good as another, they would conclude that their own moral standard has nothing special to recommend it. They might as well then slip down to some lower and easier standard. It is true that, for a time, it may be possible to hold one view in theory and to act practically upon another. But ideas, even philosophical ideas, are not so ineffectual that they can remain for ever idle in the upper chambers of the intellect. In the end they seep down to the level of practice. They get themselves acted on.

Vulgar Relativism

BERNARD WILLIAMS

Bernard Williams (b. 1929) is Knightbridge Professor of Philosophy at the University of Cambridge. His books include *Problems of the Self*, *Moral Luck*, and *Ethics and the Limits of Philosophy*.

Williams finds the doctrine of Ethical Relativism inconsistent, equivocal, and, finally, untenable. Some relativists maintain that (1) "right" means "right for a given society." They then conclude from this that (2) "It is not right for another society to condemn or interfere with any other." But are they not relying on a nonrelative sense of "right" in this case? What of those who belong to a society that thinks it right to interfere with other societies? On what grounds could the relativist condemn them?

[R]elativism, the anthropologist's heresy, [is] possibly the most absurd view to have been advanced even in moral philosophy. In its vulgar and unregenerate form (which I shall consider, since it is both the most distinctive and the most influential form) it consists of three propositions: that 'right' means (can only be coherently understood as meaning) 'right for a given society'; that 'right for a given society' is to be understood in a functionalist sense; and that

VULGAR RELATIVISM Slightly adapted from "Interlude: Relativism" (pp. 20–26), in *Morality: An Introduction to Ethics* by Bernard Williams. Copyright © 1972 by Bernard Williams. Reprinted by permission of Harper & Row, Publishers, Inc.

(therefore) it is wrong for people in one society to condemn, interfere with, etc., the values of another society. A view with a long history, it was popular with some liberal colonialists, notably British administrators in places (such as West Africa) in which white men held no land. In that historical role, it may have had, like some other muddled doctrines, a beneficent influence, though modern African nationalism may well deplore its tribalist and conservative implications.

Whatever its results, the view is clearly inconsistent, since it makes a claim in its third proposition, about what is right and wrong in one's dealings with other societies, which uses a *nonrelative* sense of 'right' not allowed for in the first proposition. The claim that human sacrifice, for instance, was 'right for' the Ashanti comes to be taken as saying that human sacrifice was right among the Ashanti, and this in turn as saying that human sacrifice among the Ashanti was right; i.e., we have no business to interfere with it. But this last is certainly not the sort of claim allowed by the theory. The most the theory can allow is the claim that it is right for (i.e., functionally valuable for) our society not to interfere with Ashanti society, and, first, this is certainly not all that was meant, and, second, is very dubiously true.

Apart from its logically unhappy attachment of a nonrelative morality of toleration or noninterference to a view of morality as relative, the theory suffers in its functionalists aspects from some notorious weaknesses of functionalism in general, notably difficulties that surround the identification of 'a society'. If 'society' is regarded as a cultural unit, identified in part through its values, then many of the functionalist propositions will cease to be empirical propositions and become bare tautologies: it is tediously a necessary condition of the survival of a group-with-certain-values that the group should retain those values. At the other extreme, the survival of a society could be understood as the survival of certain persons and their having descendants, in which case many functionalist propositions about the necessity of cultural survival will be false. When in Great Britain some Welsh nationalists speak of the survival of the Welsh language as a condition of the survival of Welsh society, they manage sometimes to convey an impression that it is a condition of the survival of Welsh people, as though the forgetting of Welsh were literally lethal.

In between these two extremes is the genuinely interesting territory, a province of informative social science, where there is room for such claims as that a given practice or belief is integrally connected with much more of a society's fabric than may appear on the surface, that it is not an excrescence, so that discouragement or modification of this may lead to much larger social change than might have been expected; or, again, that a certain set of values or institutions may be such that if they are lost, or seriously changed, the people in the society, while they may physically survive, will do so only in a deracinated and hopeless condition. Such propositions, if established, would of course be of first importance in deciding what to do; but they cannot take over the work of deciding what to do.

Here, and throughout the questions of conflict of values between societies, we need (and rarely get) some mildly realistic picture of what decisions might be being made by whom, of situations to which the considerations might be practically relevant. Of various paradigms that come to mind, one is that of conflict, such as the confrontation of other societies with Nazi Germany. Another is that of control, where (to eliminate further complications of the most obvious case, colonialism) one might take such a case as that of the relations of the central government of Ghana to residual elements of traditional Ashanti society. In neither case would functionalist propositions in themselves provide any answers at all. Still less will they where a major issue is whether a given group should be realistically or desirably regarded as 'a society' in a relevant sense, or whether its values and its future are to be integrally related to those of a larger group—as with the case of blacks in the United States.

The central confusion of relativism is to try to conjure out of the fact that societies have differing attitudes and values an *a priori* nonrelative principle to determine the attitude of one society to another; this is impossible. If we are going to say that there are ultimate moral disagreements between societies, we must include, in the matters they can disagree about, their attitudes to other moral outlooks. It is also true, however, that there are inherent features of morality that tend to make it difficult to regard a morality as applying only to a group. The element of universalization which is present in any morality, but which applies under tribal morality perhaps only to members of the tribe, progressively comes to range over persons as such. Less formally, it is essential (as was remarked earlier) to morality and its role in any society that certain sorts of reactions and motivations should be strongly internalized, and these cannot merely evaporate because one is confronted with human beings in another society. Just as *de gustibus non disputandum* is not a maxim which applies to morality, neither is 'when in Rome do as the Roman do', which is at best a principle of etiquette.

Nor is it just a case of doing as the Romans do, but of putting up with it. Here it would be a platitude to point out that of course someone who gains wider experience of the world may rightly come to regard some moral reaction of his to unfamiliar conduct as parochial and will seek to modify or discount it. There are many important distinctions to be made here between the kinds of thoughts appropriate to such a process in different cases: sometimes he may cease to regard a certain issue as a moral matter at all, sometimes he may come to see that what abroad looked the same as something he would have deplored at home was actually, in morally relevant respects, a very different thing. (Perhaps—though one can scarcely believe it—there were some missionaries or others who saw the men in a polygamous society in the light of seedy bigamists at home.) But it would be a particular moral view, and one both psychologically and morally implausible, to insist that these adaptive reactions were the only correct ones, that confronted with practices which are found and felt as inhuman, for instance, there is an *a priori* demand of acceptance. In the fascinating book by Bernal de Diaz, who went with Cortez to Mexico, there is an account of what they all felt when they came upon the sacrificial temples. This morally unpretentious collection of bravos was genuinely horrified by the Aztec practices. It would surely be absurd to regard this reaction as merely parochial or self-righteous. It rather indicated something which their conduct did not indicate, that they regarded the Indians as men rather than as wild animals.

It is fair to press this sort of case, and in general the cases of actual confrontation. 'Every society has its own standards' may be, even if confused, a sometimes useful maxim of social study; as a maxim of social study it is also painless. But what, after all, is one supposed to do if confronted with a human sacrifice?—not a real question for many of us, perhaps, but a real question for Cortez. "It wasn't their business," it may be said; "they had no right to be there anyway."

Perhaps—though this, once more, is necessarily a nonrelative moral judgment itself. But even if they had no right to be there, it is a matter for real moral argument what would *follow* from that. For if a burglar comes across the owner of the house trying to murder somebody, is he morally obliged not to interfere because he is trespassing?

None of this is to deny the obvious facts that many have interfered with other societies when they should not have done; have interfered without understanding; and have interfered often with a brutality greater than that of anything they were trying to stop. I am saying only that it cannot be a consequence of the nature of morality itself that no society ought ever to interfere with another, or that individuals from one society confronted with the practices of another ought, if rational, to react with acceptance. To draw these consequences is the characteristic (and inconsistent) step of vulgar relativism.

Trying Out One's New Sword

MARY MIDGLEY

Mary Midgley is a senior lecturer at the University of Newcastle-upon-Tyne, England. She is the author of *Beast and Man, Heart and Mind*, and *Wickedness*.

Midgley criticizes "moral isolationists" who disapprove of those who morally judge other cultures. She notes that moral isolationists disapprove less when someone from another culture passes moral judgment on *our* culture. Also, moral isolationists are inconsistent: they do

TRYING OUT ONE'S NEW SWORD From *Heart and Mind* by Mary Midgley. © M. Midgley, 1981. Reprinted by permission of St. Martin's Press, Inc.

not oppose *praising* an exotic culture. Moral judgment, says Midgley, is a human necessity. Why ban it interculturally? She points out that such a ban would not permit us to express disapproval of the samurai custom of trying out a new sword by cleanly slicing an innocent passerby in two.

All of us are, more or less, in trouble today about trying to understand cultures strange to us. We hear constantly of alien customs. We see changes in our lifetime which would have astonished our parents. I want to discuss here one very short way of dealing with this difficulty, a drastic way which many people now theoretically favour. It consists in simply denying that we can ever understand any culture except our own well enough to make judgements about it. Those who recommend this hold that the world is sharply divided into separate societies, sealed units, each with its own system of thought. They feel that the respect and tolerance due from one system to another forbids us ever to take up a critical position to any other culture. Moral judgement, they suggest, is a kind of coinage valid only in its country of origin.

I shall call this position 'moral isolationism'. I shall suggest that it is certainly not forced upon us, and indeed that it makes no sense at all. People usually take it up because they think it is a respectful attitude to other cultures. In fact, however, it is not respectful. Nobody can respect what is entirely unintelligible to them. To respect someone, we have to know enough about him to make a *favorable* judgement, however general and tentative. And we do understand people in other cultures to this extent. Otherwise a great mass of our most valuable thinking would be paralysed.

To show this, I shall take a remote example, because we shall probably find it easier to think calmly about it than we should with a contemporary one, such as female circumcision in Africa or the Chinese Cultural Revolution. The principles involved will still be the same. My example is this. There is, it seems, a verb in classical Japanese which means 'to try out one's new sword on a chance wayfarer'. (The word is *tsujigiri*, literally 'crossroads-cut'.) A samurai sword had to be tried out because, if it was to work properly, it had to slice through someone at a single blow, from the shoulder to the opposite flank. Otherwise, the warrior bungled his stroke. This could injure his honour, offend his ancestors, and even let down his emperor. So tests were needed, and wayfarers had to be expended. Any wayfarer would do—provided, of course, that he was not another Samurai. Scientists will recognize a familiar problem about the rights of experimental subjects.

Now when we hear of a custom like this, we may well reflect that we simply do not understand it; and therefore are not qualified to criticize it at all, because we are not members of that culture. But we are not members of any other culture either, except our own. So we extend the principle to cover all extraneous cultures, and we seem therefore to be moral isolationists. But this is, as we shall see, an impossible position. Let us ask what it would involve.

We must ask first: Does the isolating barrier work both ways? Are people in other cultures equally unable to criticize *us*? This question struck me sharply when I read a remark in *The Guardian* by an anthropologist about a South American Indian who had been taken into a Brazilian town for an operation, which saved his life. When he came back to his village, he made several highly critical remarks about the white Brazilians' way of life. They may very well have been justified. But the interesting point was that the anthropologist called these remarks 'a damning indictment of Western civilization'. Now the Indian had been in that town about two weeks. Was he in a position to deliver a damning indictment? Would we ourselves be qualified to delivery such an indictment on the Samurai, provided we could spend two weeks in ancient Japan? What do we really think about this?

My own impression is that we believe that outsiders can, in principle, deliver perfectly good indictments—only, it usually takes more than two weeks to make them damning. Understanding has degrees. It is not a slapdash yes-or-no matter. Intelligent outsiders can progress in it, and in some ways will be at an advantage over the locals. But if this is so, it must clearly apply to ourselves as much as anybody else.

Our next question is this: Does the isolating barrier between cultures block praise as well as blame? If I want to say that the Samurai culture has many virtues, or to praise the South American Indians, am I prevented from doing *that* by my outside status? Now, we certainly do need to praise other societies in this way. But it is hardly possible that we could praise them effectively if we could not, in principle, criticize them. Our praise would be worthless if it rested on definite grounds, if it did not flow from some understanding. Certainly we may need to praise things which we do not *fully* understand. We say 'there's something very good here, but I can't quite make out what it is yet'. This happens when we want to learn from strangers. And we can learn from strangers. But to do this we have to distinguish between those strangers who are worth learning from and those who are not. Can we then judge which is which?

This brings us to our third question: What is involved in judging? Now plainly there is no question here of sitting on a bench in a red robe and sentencing people. Judging simply means forming an opinion, and expressing it if it is called for. Is there anything wrong about this? Naturally, we ought to avoid forming—and expressing—*crude* opinions, like that of a simple-minded missionary, who might dismiss the whole Samurai culture as entirely bad, because non-Christian. But this is a different objection. The trouble with crude opinions is that they are crude, whoever forms them, not that they are formed by the wrong people. Anthropologists, after all, are outsiders quite as much as missionaries. Moral isolationism forbids us to form *any* opinions on these matters. Its ground for doing so is that we don't understand them. But there is much that we don't understand in our own culture too. This brings us to our last question: If we can't judge other cultures, can we really judge our own? Our efforts to do so will be much damaged if we are really deprived of our opinions about other societies, because these provide the range of comparison, the spectrum of alternatives against which we set what we want to understand. We would have to stop using the mirror which anthropology so helpfully holds up to us.

In short, moral isolationism would lay down a general ban on moral reasoning. Essentially, this is the programme of immoralism, and it carries a distressing logical difficulty. Immoralists like Nietzsche are actually just a rather specialized sect of moralists. They can no more afford to put moralizing out of business than smugglers can afford to abolish customs regulations. The power of moral judgement is, in fact, not a luxury, not a perverse indulgence of the self-righteous. It is a necessity. When we judge something to be bad or good, better or worse than something else, we are taking it as an example to aim at or avoid. Without opinions of this sort, we would have no framework of comparison for our own policy, no chance of profiting by other people's insights or mistakes. In this vacuum, we could form no judgements on our own actions.

Now it would be odd if Homo sapiens had really got himself into a position as bad as this—a position where his main evolutionary asset, his brain, was so little use to him. None of us is going to accept this sceptical diagnosis. We cannot do so, because our involvement in moral isolationism does not flow from apathy, but from a rather acute concern about human hypocrisy and other forms of wickedness. But we polarize that concern around a few selected moral truths. We are rightly angry with those who despise, oppress or steamroll other cultures. We think that doing these things is actually *wrong*. But this is itself a moral judgement. We could not condemn oppression and insolence if we thought that all our condemnations were just a trivial local quirk of our own culture. We could still less do it if we tried to stop judging altogether.

Real moral scepticism, in fact, could lead only to inaction, to our losing all interest in moral questions, most of all in those which concern other societies. When we discuss these things, it becomes instantly clear how far we are from doing this. Suppose, for instance, that I criticize the bisecting Samurai, that I say his behaviour is brutal. What will usually happen next is that someone will protest, will say that I have no right to make criticisms like that of another culture. But it is more unlikely that he will use this move to end the discussion of the subject. Instead, he will justify the Samurai. He will try to fill in the background, to make me understand the custom, by explaining the exalted ideals of discipline and devotion which produced it. He will probably talk of the lower value which the ancient Japanese placed on individual life generally. He may well suggest that this is a healthier attitude than our own obsession with security. He may add, too, that the wayfarers did not seriously mind being bisected, that in principle they accepted the whole arrangement.

Now an objector who talks like this is implying that it *is* possible to understand alien customs. That is just what he is trying to make me do. And he implies, too, that if I do succeed in understanding them, I shall do something better than giving up judging them. He expects me to change my present judgement to a truer one—namely, one that is favourable. And the standards I must use to do this cannot just be Samurai standards. They have to be ones current in my own culture. Ideals like discipline and devotion will not move anybody unless he himself accepts them. As it happens, neither discipline nor devotion is very popular in the West at present. Anyone who appeals to them may well have to do some more arguing to make *them* acceptable, before he can use them to explain the Samurai. But if he does succeed here, he will have persuaded us, not just that there was someting to be said for them in ancient Japan, but that there would be here as well.

Isolating barriers simply cannot arise here. If we accept something as a serious moral truth about one culture, we can't refuse to apply it—in however different an outward form—to other cultures as well, wherever circumstances admit it. If we refuse to do this, we just are not taking the other culture seriously. This becomes clear if we look at the last argument used by my objector—that of justification by consent of the victim. It is suggested that sudden bisection is quite in order, *provided* that it takes place between consenting adults. I cannot now discuss how conclusive this justification is. What I am pointing out is simply that it can only work if we believe that *consent* can make such a transaction respectable— and this is a thoroughly modern and Western idea. It would probably never occur to a Samurai; if it did, it would surprise him very much. It is *our* standard. In applying it, too, we are likely to make another typically Western demand. We shall ask for good factual evidence that the wayfarers actually do have this rather surprising taste—that they are really willing to be bisected. In applying Western standards in this way, we are not being confused or irrelevant. We are asking the questions which arise *from where we stand*, questions which we can see the sense of. We do this because asking questions which you can't see the sense of is humbug. Certainly we can extend our questioning by imaginative effort. We can come to understand other societies better. By doing so, we may make their questions our own, or we may see that they are really forms of the questions which we are asking already. This is not impossible. It is just very hard work. The obstacles which often prevent it are simply those of ordinary ignorance, laziness and prejudice.

If there were really an isolating barrier, of course, our own culture could never have been formed. It is no sealed box, but a fertile jungle of different influences—Greek, Jewish, Roman, Norse, Celtic and so forth, into which further influences are still pouring—American, Indian, Japanese, Jamaican, you name it. The moral isolationist's picture of separate, unmixable cultures is quite unreal. People who talk about British history usually stress the value of this fertilizing mix, no doubt rightly. But this is not just an odd fact about Britain. Except for the very smallest and most remote, all cultures are formed out of many streams. All have the problem of digesting and assimilating things which, at the start, they do not understand. All have the choice of learning something from this challenge, or, alternatively, of refusing to learn, and fighting it mindlessly instead.

This universal predicament has been obscured by the fact that anthropologists used to concentrate largely on very small and remote cultures, which did not seem to have this problem. These tiny societies, which had often forgotten their own history, made neat, self-contained subjects for study. No doubt it was valuable to emphasize their remoteness, their extreme strangeness, their independence of our cultural tradition. This emphasis was, I think, the root of moral isolationism. But, as the tribal studies themselves showed, even there the anthropologists were able to interpret what they saw and make judgements—often favourable—about the tribesmen. And the tribesmen, too, were quite equal to making judgements about the anthropologists—and about the tourists and Coca-Cola salesmen who followed them. Both sets of judgements, no doubt, were somewhat hasty, both have been refined in the light of further experience. A similar transaction between us and the Samurai might take even longer. But that is no reason at all for deeming it impossible. Morally as well as physically, there is only one world, and we all have to live in it.

Chapter

4

EGOISM

Of the State of Men Without Civil Society

THOMAS HOBBES

Thomas Hobbes (1588–1679) was one of the leading philosophers of the seventeenth century. He made important contributions to metaphysics and political philosophy and is known for his theory of the "social contract." The *Leviathan* is considered to be a philosophical masterpiece.

Hobbes holds that all human beings seek to preserve and to gratify themselves. Without society they would dwell in a "state of nature," living in fear and engaged in a war of all against all. Life would be "solitary, poor, nasty, brutish, and short." Persons in the state of nature would have the "right of nature" to preserve themselves by whatever means necessary. But no individual in this natural state would be strong enough to feel secure; so it is to *everyone's* benefit to obtain a measure of security by forming a society in which one gives up one's freedom to do as one pleases. In society one places oneself under a sovereign. In return for this, one receives the security afforded by sovereign protection.

This selection presents Hobbes's classic description of human beings in the state of nature. It explains why it would be rational for self-seeking individuals to curb their untrammeled egoism by entering into a lawful community.

OF THE STATE OF MEN WITHOUT CIVIL SOCIETY   From *De Cive* by Thomas Hobbes, chapter 2.

1. The faculties of human nature may be reduced unto four kinds; bodily strength, experience, reason, passion. Taking the beginning of this following doctrine from these, we will declare in the first place what manner of inclinations men who are endued with these faculties bear towards each other, and whether, and by what faculty they are born, apt for society, and to preserve themselves against mutual violence; then proceeding, we will shew what advice was necessary to be taken for this business, and what are the conditions of society, or of human peace; that is to say, (changing the words only) what are the fundamental laws of nature.

2. The greatest part of those men who have written aught concerning commonwealths, either suppose, or require us, or beg of us to believe, that man is a creature born fit for society. The Greeks call him ζῶον πολιτικόν; and on this foundation they so build up the doctrine of civil society, as if for the preservation of peace, and the government of mankind, there were nothing else necessary, than that men should agree to make certain covenants and conditions together, which themselves should then call laws. Which axiom, though received by most, is yet certainly false, and an error proceeding from our too slight contemplation of human nature. For they who shall more narrowly look into the causes for which men come together, and delight in each other's company, shall easily find that this happens not because naturally it could happen no otherwise, but by accident. For if by nature one man should love another (that is) as man, there could no reason be returned why every man should not equally love every man, as being equally man, or why he should rather frequent those whose society affords him honour or profit. We do not therefore by nature seek society for its own sake, but that we may receive some honour or profit from it; these we desire primarily, that secondarily. How, by what advice, men do meet, will be best known by observing those things which they do when they are met. For if they meet for traffic, it is plain every man regards not his fellow, but his business; if to discharge some office, a certain market-friendship is begotten, which hath more of jealousy in it than true love, and whence factions sometimes may arise, but good will never; if for pleasure, and recreation of mind, every man is wont to please himself most with those things which stir up laughter, whence he may (according to the nature of that which is ridiculous) by comparison of another man's defects and infirmities, pass the more current in his

169

own opinion; and although this be sometimes innocent and without offence, yet it is manifest they are not so much delighted with the society, as their own vain glory. But for the most part, in these kinds of meetings, we wound the absent; their whole life, sayings, actions are examined, judged, condemned; nay, it is very rare, but some present receive a fling before they part, so as his reason was not ill, who was wont always at parting to go out last. And these are indeed the true delights of society, unto which we are carried by nature, that is, by those passions which are incident to all creatures, until either by sad experience, or good precepts, it so fall out (which in many never happens) that the appetite of present matters be dulled with the memory of things past, without which, the discourse of most quick and nimble men on this subject, is but cold and hungry.

But if it so happen, that being met, they pass their time in relating some stories, and one of them begins to tell one which concerns himself; instantly every one of the rest most greedily desires to speak of himself too; if one relate some wonder, the rest will tell you miracles, if they have them, if not, they will feign them. Lastly, that I may say somewhat of them who pretend to be wiser than others; if they meet to talk of philosophy, look how many men, so many would be esteemed masters, or else they not only love not their fellows, but even persecute them with hatred. So clear is it by experience to all men who a little more narrowly consider human affairs, that all free congress ariseth either from mutual poverty, or from vain glory, whence the parties met, endeavour to carry with them either some benefit, or to leave behind them that same εὐδοκιμεῖν some esteem and honour with those, with whom they have been conversant. The same is also collected by reason out of the definitions themselves, of will, good, honour, profitable. For when we voluntarily contract society, in all manner of society we look after the object of the will, that is, that, which every one of those who gather together, propounds to himself for good. Now whatsoever seems good, is pleasant, and relates either to the senses, or the mind. But all the mind's pleasure is either glory, (or to have a good opinion of one's self) or refers to glory in the end; the rest are sensual, or conducing to sensuality, which may be all comprehended under the word conveniences. All society therefore is either for gain, or for glory; that is, not so much for love of our fellows, as for the love of ourselves. But no society can be great, or lasting, which begins from vain glory; because that glory is like honour, if all men have it, no man hath it, for they consist in comparison and precellence; neither doth the society of others advance any whit the cause of my glorying in myself; for every man must account himself, such as he can make himself, without the help of others. But though the benefits of this life may be much farthered by mutual help, since yet those may be better attained to by dominion, than by the society of others: I hope no body will doubt but that men would much more greedily be carried by nature, if all fear were removed, to obtain dominion, than to gain society. We must therefore resolve, that the original of all great and lasting societies consisted not in the mutual good will men had towards each other, but in the mutual fear they had of each other.

3. The cause of mutual fear consists partly in the natural equality of men, partly in their mutual will of hurting: whence it comes to pass, that we can neither expect from others, nor promise to ourselves the least security. For if we look on men full-grown, and consider how brittle the frame of our human body is, which perishing, all its strength, vigour, and wisdom itself perisheth with it; and how easy a matter it is, even for the weakest man to kill the strongest: there is no reason why any man, trusting to his own strength, should conceive himself made by nature above others. They are equals, who can do equal things one against the other; but they who can do the greatest things, namely, kill, can do equal things. All men therefore among themselves are by nature equal; the inequality we now discern, hath its spring from the civil law.

4. All men in the state of nature have a desire and will to hurt, but not proceeding from the same cause, neither equally to be condemned. For one man, according to that natural equality which is among us, permits as much to others as he assumes to himself; which is an argument of a temperate man, and one that rightly values his power. Another, supposing himself above others, will have a license to do what he lists, and challenges respect and honour, as due to him before others; which is an argument of a fiery spirit. This man's will to hurt ariseth from vain glory, and the false esteem he hath of his own strength; the other's from the necessity of defending himself, his liberty, and his goods, against this man's violence.

5. Furthermore, since the combat of wits is the fiercest, the

greatest discords which are, must necessarily arise from this contention. For in this case it is not only odious to contend against, but also not to consent. For not to approve of what a man saith, is no less than tacitly to accuse him of an error in that thing which he speaketh; as in very many things to dissent, is as much as if you accounted him a fool whom you dissent from; which may appear hence, that there are no wars so sharply waged as between sects of the same religion, and factions of the same commonweal, where the contestation is either concerning doctrines or politic prudence. And since all the pleasure and jollity of the mind consists in this, even to get some, with whom comparing, it may find somewhat wherein to triumph and vaunt itself; it is impossible but men must declare sometimes some mutual scorn and contempt, either by laughter, or by words, or by gesture, or some sign or other; than which there is no greater vexation of mind, and than from which there cannot possibly arise a greater desire to do hurt.

6. But the most frequent reason why men desire to hurt each other, ariseth hence, that many men at the same time have an appetite to the same thing; which yet very often they can neither enjoy in common, nor yet divide it; whence it follows that the strongest must have it, and who is strongest must be decided by the sword.

7. Among so many dangers therefore, as the natural lusts of men do daily threaten each other withal, to have a care of one's self is not a matter so scornfully to be looked upon, as if so be there had not been a power and will left in one to have done otherwise. For every man is desirous of what is good for him, and shuns what is evil, but chiefly the chiefest of natural evils, which is death; and this he doth, by a certain impulsion of nature, no less than that whereby a stone moves downward. It is therefore neither absurd, nor reprehensible, neither against the dictates of true reason, for a man to use all his endeavours to preserve and defend his body and the members thereof from death and sorrows. But that which is not contrary to right reason, that all men account to be done justly, and with right; neither by the word right is anything else signified, than that liberty which every man hath to make use of his natural faculties according to right reason. Therefore the first foundation of natural right is this, that every man as much as in him lies endeavour to protect his life and members.

8. But because it is in vain for a man to have a right to the end,

if the right to the necessary means be denied him; it follows, that since every man hath a right to preserve himself, he must also be allowed a right to use all the means, and do all the actions, without which he cannot preserve himself.

9.   Now whether the means which he is about to use, and the action he is performing, be necessary to the preservation of his life and members, or not, he himself, by the right of nature, must be judge. For say another man judge that it is contrary to right reason that I should judge of mine own peril: why now, because he judgeth of what concerns me, by the same reason, because we are equal by nature, will I judge also of things which do belong to him. Therefore it agrees with right reason, that is, it is the right of nature that I judge of his opinion, that is, whether it conduce to my preservation, or not.

10.   Nature hath given to every one a right to all; that is, it was lawful for every man in the bare state of nature, or before such time as men had engaged themselves by any covenants or bonds, to do what he would, and against whom he thought fit, and to possess, use, and enjoy all what he would, or could get. Now because whatsoever a man would, it therefore seems good to him because he wills it, and either it really doth, or at least seems to him to contribute towards his preservation, (but we have already allowed him to be judge, in the foregoing article, whether it doth or not, in so much as we are to hold all for necessary whatsoever he shall esteem so), and by the 7th article it appears that by the right of nature those things may be done, and must be had, which necessarily conduce to the protection of life and members, it follows, that in the state of nature, to have all, and do all, is lawful for all. And this is that which is meant by that common saying, nature hath given all to all, from whence we understand likewise, that in the state of nature, profit is the measure of right.

11.   But it was the least benefit for men thus to have a common right to all things; for the effects of this right are the same, almost, as if there had been no right at all. For although any man might say of every thing, this is mine, yet could he not enjoy it, by reason of his neighbour, who having equal right, and equal power, would pretend the same thing to be his.

12.   If now to this natural proclivity of men, to hurt each other, which they derive from their passions, but chiefly from a vain esteem of themselves, you add, the right of all to all, wherewith

one by right invades, the other by right resists, and whence arise perpetual jealousies and suspicions on all hands, and how hard a thing it is to provide against an enemy invading us, with an intention to oppress, and ruin, though he come with a small number, and no great provision; it cannot be denied but that the natural state of men, before they entered into society, was a mere war, and that not simply, but a war of all men against all men. For what is war, but that same time in which the will of contesting by force is fully declared, either by words, or deeds? The time remaining, is termed peace.

13. But it is easily judged how disagreeable a thing to the preservation either of mankind, or of each single man, a perpetual war is. But it is perpetual in its own nature, because in regard of the equality of those that strive, it cannot be ended by victory; for in this state the conqueror is subject to so much danger, as it were to be accounted a miracle, if any, even the most strong, should close up his life with many years, and old age. They of America are examples hereof, even in this present age: other nations have been in former ages, which now indeed are become civil and flourishing, but were then few, fierce, short-lived, poor, nasty, and deprived of all that pleasure, and beauty of life, which peace and society are wont to bring with them. Whosoever therefore holds, that it had been best to have continued in that state in which all things were lawful for all men, he contradicts himself. For every man by natural necessity desires that which is good for him: nor is there any that esteems a war of all against all, which necessarily adheres to such a state, to be good for him. And so it happens, that through fear of each other we think it fit to rid ourselves of this condition, and to get some fellows; that if there needs must be war, it may not yet be against all men, nor without some helps.

14. Fellows are gotten either by constraint, or by consent; by constraint, when after fight the conqueror makes the conquered serve him, either through fear of death, or by laying fetters on him: by consent, when men enter into society to help each other, both parties consenting without any constraint. But the conqueror may by right compel the conquered, or the strongest the weaker, (as a man in health may one that is sick, or he that is of riper years a child), unless he will choose to die, to give caution of his future obedience. For since the right of protecting ourselves according to our own wills, proceeded from our danger, and our danger from

our equality, it is more consonant to reason, and more certain for our conservation, using the present advantage to secure ourselves by taking caution, than when they shall be full grown and strong, and got out of our power, to endeavour to recover that power again by doubtful fight. And on the other side, nothing can be thought more absurd, than by discharging whom you already have weak in your power, to make him at once both an enemy and a strong one. From whence we may understand likewise as a corollary in the natural state of men, that, *a sure and irresistible power confers the right of dominion and ruling over those who cannot resist*; insomuch, as the right of all things that can be done, adheres essentially and immediately unto this omnipotence hence arising.

15.   Yet cannot men expect any lasting preservation, continuing thus in the state of nature, that is, of war, by reason of that equality of power, and other human faculties they are endued withal. Wherefore to seek peace, where there is any hopes of obtaining it, and where there is none, to enquire out for auxiliaries of war, is the dictate of right reason, that is, the law of nature.

The Virtue of Selfishness

AYN RAND

Ayn Rand (1905–1982) is a well-known novelist and social thinker. Her best-known novels are *Atlas Shrugged* and *The Fountainhead*. Her nonfiction works include *For the New Intellectual* and *Capitalism: The Unknown Ideal*.

Rand defines selfishness as "concern with one's own interests," and she asks why this should be considered a vice. Altruism, the selfless pursuit of the good of others, is a dangerous ideal that engenders guilt and cynicism in those who seek to practice it and impose it on others. "Cynicism, because they neither practice nor accept the

THE VIRTUE OF SELFISHNESS   From the Introduction to *Virtue of Selfishness*. Reprinted by permission of Leonard Peikoff, Executor, Estate of Ayn Rand.

altruist morality—guilt, because they dare not reject it."
Rand believes that a responsible concern for one's own
interests is the essence of a moral existence.

The title of this book may evoke the kind of question that I hear once in a while: "Why do you use the word 'selfishness' to denote virtuous qualities of character, when that word antagonizes so many people to whom it does not mean the things you mean?"

To those who ask it, my answer is: "For the reason that makes you afraid of it."

But there are others, who would not ask that question, sensing the moral cowardice it implies, yet who are unable to formulate my actual reason or to identify the profound moral issue involved. It is to them that I will give a more explicit answer.

It is not a mere semantic issue nor a matter of arbitrary choice. The meaning ascribed in popular usage to the word "selfishness" is not merely wrong: it represents a devastating intellectual "package-deal," which is responsible, more than any other single factor, for the arrested moral development of mankind.

In popular usage, the word "selfishness" is a synonym of evil; the image it conjures is of a murderous brute who tramples over piles of corpses to achieve his own ends, who cares for no living being and pursues nothing but the gratification of the mindless whims of any immediate moment.

Yes the exact meaning and dictionary definition of the word "selfishness" is: *concern with one's own interests.*

This concept does *not* include a moral evaluation; it does not tell us whether concern with one's own interests is good or evil; nor does it tell us what constitutes man's actual interests. It is the task of ethics to answer such questions.

The ethics of altruism has created the image of the brute, as its answer, in order to make men accept two inhuman tenets: (a) that any concern with one's own interests is evil, regardless of what these interests might be, and (b) that the brute's activities are *in fact* to one's own interest (which altruism enjoins man to renounce for the sake of his neighbors).

For a view of the nature of altruism, its consequences and the enormity of the moral corruption it perpetrates, I shall refer you to

Atlas Shrugged—or to any of today's newspaper headlines. What concerns us here is altruism's *default* in the field of ethical theory.

There are two moral questions which altruism lumps together into one "package-deal": (1) What are values? (2) Who should be the beneficiary of values? Altruism substitutes the second for the first; it evades the task of defining a code of moral values, thus leaving man, in fact, without moral guidance.

Altruism declares that any action taken for the benefit of others is good, and any action taken for one's own benefit is evil. Thus the *beneficiary* of an action is the only criterion of moral value—and so long as the beneficiary is anybody other than oneself, anything goes.

Hence the appalling immorality, the chronic injustice, the grotesque double standards, the insoluble conflicts and contradictions that have characterized human relationships and human societies throughout history, under all the variants of the altruist ethics.

Observe the indecency of what passes for moral judgments today. An industrialist who produces a fortune, and a gangster who robs a bank are regarded as equally immoral, since they both sought wealth for their own "selfish" benefit. A young man who gives up his career in order to support his parents and never rises beyond the rank of grocery clerk is regarded as morally superior to the young man who endures an excruciating struggle and achieves his personal ambition. A dictator is regarded as moral, since the unspeakable atrocities he committed were intended to benefit "the people," not himself.

Observe what this beneficiary-criterion of morality does to a man's life. The first thing he learns is that morality is his enemy: he has nothing to gain from it, he can only lose; self-inflicted loss, self-inflicted pain and the gray, debilitating pall of an incomprehensible duty is all that he can expect. He may hope that others might occasionally sacrifice themselves for his benefit, as he grudgingly sacrifices himself for theirs, but he knows that the relationship will bring mutual resentment, not pleasure—and that, morally, their pursuit of values will be like an exchange of unwanted, unchosen Christmas presents, which neither is morally permitted to buy for himself. Apart from such times as he manages to perform some act of self-sacrifice, he possesses no moral significance: morality takes no cognizance of him and has nothing to say to him for guidance in the crucial issues of his life; it is only his own

177

personal, private, "selfish" life and, as such, it is regarded either as evil or, at best, *amoral*.

Since nature does not provide man with an automatic form of survival, since he has to support his life by his own effort, the doctrine that concern with one's own interests is evil means that man's desire to live is evil—that man's life, as such, is evil. No doctrine could be more evil than that.

Yet that is the meaning of altruism, implicit in such examples as the equation of an industrialist with a robber. There is a fundamental moral difference between a man who sees his self-interest in production and a man who sees it in robbery. The evil of a robber does *not* lie in the fact that he pursues his own interests, but in *what* he regards as to his own interest; *not* in the fact that he pursues his values, but in *what* he chose to value; *not* in the fact that he wants to live, but in the fact that he wants to live on a sub-human level. . . .

If it is true that what I mean by "selfishness" is not what is meant conventionally, then *this* is one of the worst indictments of altruism: it means that altruism *permits no concept* of a self-respecting, self-supporting man—a man who supports his life by his own effort and neither sacrifices himself nor others. It means that altruism permits no view of men except as sacrificial animals and profiteers-on-sacrifice, as victims and parasites—that it permits no concept of a benevolent coexistence among men—that it permits no concept of *justice*.

If you wonder about the reasons behind the ugly mixture of cynicism and guilt in which most men spend their lives, these are the reasons: cynicism, because they neither practice nor accept the altruist morality—guilt, because they dare not reject it.

To rebel against so devastating an evil, one has to rebel against its basic premise. To redeem both man and morality, it is the concept of *"selfishness"* that one has to redeem.

Egoism and Moral Skepticism

JAMES RACHELS

James Rachels (b. 1941) is the dean of the School of Humanities at the University of Alabama. He is the editor of several books, including *Moral Problems: A Collection of Philosophical Essays* and *Understanding Moral Philosophy*.

Psychological egoism is the view that human being always act from a single motive: self-love. Ethical egoism is the moral theory that says we *ought* to act only from self-love. Rachels tries to expose the logical and moral weaknesses of both theories. For example, he challenges the view often proffered by defenders of psychological egoism: we are selfish because we *always do what we want to do*. One person *wants* to visit and cheer up a lonely elderly neighbor; another wants to rob and terrorize a neighbor. Both do what they want; both are selfish. Rachels points out that what makes an act selfish is its *object*, not that one wants to do it. If the object of most of our actions is to please ourselves, then we are selfish; if we often want to please our neighbors, we are kind. If we want to harm them, we are malicious. Rachels also argues that both psychological and ethical egoisms rest upon a distorted view of human nature. Most of us are

EGOISM AND MORAL SKEPTICISM From *A New Introduction to Philosophy*, edited by Steven M. Cahn. Copyright © 1971 by Steven M. Cahn. Reprinted by permission of Harper & Row, Publishers, Inc.

sympathetic and care about the well-being of others. The reason we do not burn down a department store is not because it might not be in our long-range interest to do so, but because "people might be burned to death."

I

Our ordinary thinking about morality is full of assumptions that we almost never question. We assume, for example, that we have an obligation to consider the welfare of other people when we decide what actions to perform or what rules to obey; we think that we must refrain from acting in ways harmful to others, and that we must respect their rights and interests as well as our own. We also assume that people are in fact capable of being motivated by such considerations, that is, that people are not wholly selfish and that they do sometimes act in the interests of others.

Both of these assumptions have come under attack by moral skeptics, as long ago as by Glaucon in Book II of Plato's *Republic*. Glaucon recalls the legend of Gyges, a shepherd who was said to have found a magic ring in a fissure opened by an earthquake. The ring would make its wearer invisible and thus would enable him to go anywhere and do anything undetected. Gyges used the power of the ring to gain entry to the Royal Palace where he seduced the Queen, murdered the King, and subsequently seized the throne. Now Glaucon asks us to determine that there are two such rings, one given to a man of virtue and one given to a rogue. The rogue, of course, will use his ring unscrupulously and do anything necessary to increase his own wealth and power. He will recognize no moral constraints on his conduct, and, since the cloak of invisibility will protect him from discovery, he can do anything he pleases without fear of reprisal. So there will be no end to the mischief he will do. But how will the so-called virtuous man behave? Glaucon suggests that he will behave no better than the rogue: "No one, it is commonly believed, would have such iron strength of mind as to stand fast in doing right or keep his hands off other men's goods, when he could go the market-place and fearlessly help himself to anything he wanted, enter houses and sleep with any woman he chose, set prisoners free and kill men at his pleasure, and in a word go about among men with the powers of a god. He would behave no better than the other; both would take the same course."[1] Moreover, why shouldn't he? Once he is freed from the fear of reprisal, why shouldn't a man simply do what he pleases, or what he thinks is best for himself? What reason is there for him to continue being "moral" when it is clearly not to his own advantage to do so?

These skeptical views suggested by Glaucon have come to be known as *psychological egoism* and *ethical egoism* respectively. Psychological egoism is the view that all men are selfish in every-thing that they do, that is, that the only motive from which anyone ever acts is self-interest. On this view, even when men are acting in ways apparently calculated to benefit others, they are actually moti-vated by the belief that acting in this way is to their own advantage, and if they did not believe this, they would not be doing that action. Ethical egoism is, by contrast, a normative view about how men *ought* to act. It is the view that, regardless of how men do in fact behave, they have no obligation to do anything except what is in their own interests. According to the ethical egoist, a person is always justified in doing whatever is in his own interest, regardless of the effect on others.

Clearly, if either of these views is correct, then "the moral institution of life" (to use Butler's well-turned phrase) is very different than what we normally think. The majority of mankind is grossly deceived about what is, or ought to be, the case, where morals are concerned.

II

Psychological egoism seems to fly in the face of the facts. We are tempted to say, "Of course people act unselfishly all the time. For example, Smith gives up a trip to the country, which he would have enjoyed very much, in order to stay behind and help a friend with his studies, which is a miserable way to pass the time. This is a perfectly clear case of unselfish behavior, and if the psychological egoist thinks that such cases do not occur, then he is just mistaken." Given such obvious instances of "unselfish behavior," what reply can the egoist make? There are two general arguments by which he

---

[1] *The Republic of Plato*, trans. F. M. Cornford (Oxford, 1941), p. 45.

might try to show that all actions, including those such as the one just outlined, are in fact motivated by self-interest. Let us examine these in turn:

A. The first argument goes as follows. If we describe one person's action as selfish, and another person's action as unselfish, we are overlooking the crucial fact that in both cases, assuming that the action is done voluntarily, *the agent is merely doing what he most wants to do.* If Smith stays behind to help his friend, that only shows that he wanted to help his friend more than he wanted to go to the country. And why should he be praised for his "unselfishness" when he is only doing what he most wants to do? So, since Smith is only doing what he wants to do, he cannot be said to be acting unselfishly.

This argument is so bad that it would not deserve to be taken seriously except for the fact that so many otherwise intelligent people have been taken in by it. First, the argument rests on the premise that people never voluntarily do anything except what they want to do. But this is patently false; there are at least two classes of actions that are exceptions to this generalization. One is the set of actions which we may not want to do, but which we do anyway as a means to an end which we want to achieve; for example, going to the dentist in order to stop a toothache, or going to work every day in order to be able to draw our pay at the end of the month. These cases may be regarded as consistent with the spirit of the egoist argument, however, since the ends mentioned are wanted by the agent. But the other set of actions are those which we do, not because we want to, nor even because there is an end which we want to achieve, but because we feel ourselves *under an obligation* to do them. For example, someone may do something because he has promised to do it, and thus feels obligated, even though he does not want to do it. It is sometimes suggested that in such cases we do the action because, after all, we want to keep our promises; so, even here, we are doing what we want. However, this dodge will not work: If I have promised to do something, and if I do not want to do it, then it is simply false to say that I want to keep my promise. In such cases we feel a conflict precisely because we do *not* want to do what we feel obligated to do. It is reasonable to think that Smith's action falls roughly into this second category: He might stay behind, not because he wants to, but because he feels that his friend needs help.

182

But suppose we were to concede, for the sake of the argument, that all voluntary action is motivated by the agent's wants, or at least that Smith is so motivated. Even if these were granted, it would not follow that Smith is acting selfishly or from self-interest. For if Smith wants to do something that will help his friend, even when it means foregoing his own enjoyments, that is precisely what makes him *unselfish*. What else could unselfishness be, if not wanting to help others? Another way to put the same point is to say that it is the *object* of a want that determines whether it is selfish or not. The mere fact that I am acting on *my* wants does not mean that I am acting selfishly; that depends on *what it is* that I want. If I want only my own good, and care nothing for others, then I am selfish; but if I also want other people to be well-off and happy, and if I act on *that* desire, then my action is not selfish. So much for this argument.

B. The second argument for psychological egoism is this. Since so-called unselfish actions always produce a sense of self-satisfaction in the agent,[2] and since this sense of satisfaction is a pleasant state of consciousness, it follows that the point of the action is really to achieve a pleasant state of consciousness, rather than to bring about any good for others. Therefore, the action is "unselfish" only at a superficial level of analysis. Smith will feel much better with himself for having stayed to help his friend—if he had gone to the country, he would have felt terrible about it—and that is the real point of the action. According to a well-known story, this argument was once expressed by Abraham Lincoln:

> Mr. Lincoln once remarked to a fellow-passenger on an old-time mud-coach that all men were prompted by selfishness in doing good. His fellow-passenger was antagonizing this position when they were passing over a corduroy bridge that spanned a slough. As they crossed this bridge they espied an old razor-backed sow on the bank making a terrible noise because her pigs had got into the slough and were in danger of drowning. As the old coach began to climb the hill, Mr. Lincoln called out, "Driver, can't you stop just a moment?" Then Mr. Lincoln jumped out, ran back, and lifted the little pigs out of the mud and water and placed them on the bank.

---

[2] Or, as it is sometimes said, "It gives him a clear conscience," or "He couldn't sleep at night if he had done otherwise," or "He would have been ashamed of himself for not doing it," and so on.

When he returned, his companion remarked: "Now Abe, where does selfishness come in on this little episode?" "Why, bless your soul, Ed, that was the very essence of selfishness. I should have had no peace of mind all day had I gone on and left that suffering old sow worrying over those pigs. I did it to get peace of mind, don't you see?"[3]

This argument suffers from defects similar to the previous one. Why should we think that merely because someone derives satisfaction from helping others this makes him selfish? Isn't the unselfish man precisely the one who *does* derive satisfaction from helping others, while the selfish man does not? If Lincoln "got peace of mind" from rescuing the piglets, does this show him to be selfish, or, on the contrary, doesn't it show him to be compassionate and good-hearted? (If a man were truly selfish, why should it bother his conscience that *others* suffer—much less pigs?) Similarly, it is nothing more than shabby sophistry to say, because Smith takes satisfaction in helping his friend, that he is behaving selfishly. If we say this rapidly, while thinking about something else, perhaps it will sound all right; but if we speak slowly, and pay attention to what we are saying, it sounds plain silly.

Moreover, suppose we ask *why* Smith derives satisfaction from helping his friend. The answer will be, it is because Smith cares for him and wants him to succeed. If Smith did not have these concerns, then he would take no pleasure in assisting him; and these concerns, as we have already seen, are the marks of unselfishness, not selfishness. To put the point more generally: If we have a positive attitude toward the attainment of some goal, then we may derive satisfaction from attaining that goal. But the *object* of our attitude is *the attainment of that goal*; and we must want to attain the goal *before* we can find any satisfaction in it. We do not, in other words, desire some sort of "pleasurable consciousness" and then try to figure out how to achieve it; rather, we desire all sorts of different things—money, a new fishing-boat, to be a better chess-player, to get a promotion in our work, etc.—and because we desire these things, we derive satisfaction from attaining them. And

[3]Frank C. Sharp, *Ethics* (New York, 1928), pp. 74–75. Quoted from the Springfield (Ill.) *Monitor* in the *Outlook*, vol. 56, p. 1059.

so, if someone desires the welfare and happiness of another person, he will derive satisfaction from that; but this does not mean that this satisfaction is the object of his desire, or that he is in any way selfish on account of it.

It is a measure of the weakness of psychological egoism that these insupportable arguments are the ones most often advanced in its favor. Why, then, should anyone ever have thought it a true view? Perhaps because of a desire for theoretical simplicity: In thinking about human conduct, it would be nice if there were some simple formula that would unite the diverse phenomena of human behavior under a single explanatory principle, just as simple formulae in physics bring together a great many apparently different phenomena. And since it is obvious that self-regard is an overwhelmingly important factor in motivation, it is only natural to wonder whether all motivation might not be explained in these terms. But the answer is clearly No; while a great many human actions are motivated entirely or in part by self-interest, only by a deliberate distortion of the facts can we say that all conduct is so motivated. This will be clear, I think, if we correct three confusions which are commonplace. The exposure of these confusions will remove the last traces of plausibility from the psychological egoist thesis.

The first is the confusion of selfishness with self-interest. The two are clearly not the same. If I see a physician when I am feeling poorly, I am acting in my own interest but no one would think of calling me "selfish" on account of it. Similarly, brushing my teeth, working hard at my job, and obeying the law are all in my self-interest but none of these are examples of selfish conduct. This is because selfish behavior is behavior that ignores the interests of others, in circumstances in which their interests ought not to be ignored. This concept has a definite evaluative flavor; to call someone "selfish" is not just to describe his action but to condemn it. Thus, you would not call me selfish for eating a normal meal in normal circumstances (although it may surely be in my self-interest); but you would call me selfish for hoarding food while others about are starving.

The second confusion is the assumption that every action is done *either* from self-interest or from other-regarding motives. Thus, the egoist concludes that if there is no such thing as genuine altruism then all actions must be done from self-interest. But this is certainly a false dichotomy. The man who continues to smoke cigarettes, even after learning about the connection between smoking and cancer, is surely not acting from self-interest, not even by his own standards—self-interest would dictate that he quit smoking at once—and he is not acting altruistically either. He *is*, no doubt, smoking for the pleasure of it, but all that this shows is that undisciplined pleasure-seeking and acting from self-interest are very different. This is what led Butler to remark that "The thing to be lamented is, not that men have so great regard to their own good or interest in the present world, for they have not enough."[4]

The last two paragraphs show (*a*) that it is false that all actions are selfish, and (*b*) that it is false that all actions are done out of self-interest. And it should be noted that these two points can be made, and were, without any appeal to putative examples of altruism.

The third confusion is the common but false assumption that a concern for one's own welfare is incompatible with any genuine concern for the welfare of others. Thus, since it is obvious that everyone (or very nearly everyone) does desire his own well-being, it might be thought that no one can really be concerned with others. But again, this is false. There is no inconsistency in desiring that everyone, including oneself *and* others, be well-off and happy. To be sure, it may happen on occasion that our own interests conflict with the interests of others, and in these cases we will have to make hard choices. But even in these cases we might sometimes opt for the interests of others, especially when the others involved are our family or friends. But more importantly, not all cases are like this: Sometimes we are able to promote the welfare of others when our own interests are not involved at all. In these cases not even the strongest self-regard need prevent us from acting considerately toward others.

Once these confusions are cleared away, it seems to me obvious enough that there is no reason whatever to accept psychological egoism. On the contrary, if we simply observe people's behavior with an open mind, we may find that a great deal of it is motivated by self-regard, but by no means all of it; and that there is no reason

---

[4]*The Works of Joseph Butler*, ed. W. E. Gladstone (Oxford, 1896), vol. 2, p. 26.

to deny that "the moral institution of life" can include a place for the virtue of beneficence.[5]

III

The ethical egoist would say at this point, "Of course it is possible for people to act altruistically, and perhaps many people do act that way—but there is no reason why they *should* do so. A person is under no obligation to do anything except what is in his own interests."[6] This is really quite a radical doctrine. Suppose I have an urge to set fire to some public building (say, a department store) just for the fascination of watching the spectacular blaze: According to this view, the fact that several people might be burned to death provides no reason whatever why I should not do it. After all, this only concerns *their* welfare, not my own, and according to the ethical egoist the only person I need think of is myself.

Some might deny that ethical egoism has any such monstrous consequences. They would point out that it is really to my own advantage not to set the fire—for, if I do that I may be caught and put into prison (unlike Gyges, I have no magic ring for protection). Moreover, even if I could avoid being caught it is still to my advantage to respect the rights and interests of others, for it is to my advantage to live in a society in which people's rights and interests are respected. Only in such a society can I live a happy and secure life; so, in acting kindly toward others, I would merely be doing my part to create and maintain the sort of society which it is to my advantage to have.[7] Therefore, it is said, the egoist would not be such a bad man; he would be as kindly and considerate as anyone else, because he would see that it is to his own advantage to be kindly and considerate.

This is a seductive line of thought, but it seems to me mistaken. Certainly it is to everyone's advantage (including the egoist's) to

---

[5] The capacity for altruistic behavior is not unique to human beings. Some interesting experiments with rhesus monkeys have shown that these animals will refrain from operating a device for securing food if this causes other animals to suffer pain. See Masserman, Wechkin, and Terris, "'Altruistic' Behavior in Rhesus Monkeys," *the American Journal of Psychiatry*, vol. 121 (1964), 584–585.

[6] I take this to be the view of Ayn Rand, insofar as I understand her confusing doctrine.

[7] Cf. Thomas Hobbes, *Leviathan* (London, 1651), chap. 17.

preserve a stable society where people's interests are generally protected. But there is no reason for the egoist to think that merely because *he* will not honor the rules of the social game, decent society will collapse. For the vast majority of people are not egoists, and there is no reason to think that they will be converted by his example—especially if he is discreet and does not unduly flaunt his style of life. What this line of reasoning shows is not that the egoist himself must act benevolently, but that he must encourage *others* to do so. He must take care to conceal from public view his own self-centered method of decision-making, and urge others to act on precepts very different from those on which he is willing to act.

The rational egoist, then, cannot advocate that egoism be universally adopted by everone. For he wants a world in which his own interests are maximized; and if other people adopted the egoistic policy of pursuing their own interests to the exclusion of his interest, as he pursues his interests to the exclusion of theirs, then such a world would be impossible. So he himself will be egoist, but he will want others to be altruists.

This brings us to what is perhaps the most popular "refutation" of ethical egoism current among philosophical writers—the argument that ethical egoism is at bottom inconsistent because it cannot be universalized.[8] The argument goes like this:

To say that any action or policy of action is *right* (or that it *ought* to be adopted) entails that it is right for *anyone* in the same sort of circumstances. I cannot, for example, say that it is right for me to lie to you, and yet object when you lie to me (provided, of course, that the circumstances are the same). I cannot hold that it is all right for me to drink your beer and then complain when you drink mine. This is just the requirement that we be consistent in our evaluations; it is a requirement of logic. Now it is said that ethical egoism cannot meet this requirement because, as we have already seen, the egoist would not want others to act in the same way that he acts. Moreover, suppose he *did* advocate the universal adoption of egoistic policies: he would be saying to Peter, "You ought to

[8]See, for example, Brian Medlin, "Ultimate Principles and Ethical Egoism," *Australasian Journal of Philosophy*, vol. 35 (1957), 111–118; and D. H. Monro, *Empiricism and Ethics* (Cambridge, 1967), chap. 16.

pursue your own interests even if it means destroying Paul"; and he would be saying to Paul, "You ought to pursue your own interests even if it means destroying Peter." The attitudes expressed in these two recommendations seem clearly inconsistent—he is urging the advancement of Peter's interest at one moment, and countenancing their defeat at the next. Therefore, the argument goes, there is no way to maintain the doctrine of ethical egoism as a consistent view about how we ought to act. We will fall into inconsistency whenever we try.

What are we to make of this argument? Are we to conclude that ethical egoism has been refuted? Such a conclusion, I think, would be unwarranted; for I think that we can show, contrary to this argument, how ethical egoism can be maintained consistently. We need only to interpret the egoist's position in a sympathetic way: We should say that he has in mind a certain kind of world which he would prefer over all others; it would be a world in which his own interests were maximized, regardless of the effects on other people. The egoist's primary policy of action, then, would be to act in such a way as to bring about, as nearly as possible, this sort of world. Regardless of however morally reprehensible we might find it, there is nothing *inconsistent* in someone's adopting this as his ideal and acting in a way calculated to bring it about. And if someone did adopt this as his ideal, then he would not advocate universal egoism; as we have already seen, he would want other people to be altruists. So if he advocates any principles of conduct for the general public, they will be altruistic principles. This would not be inconsistent; on the contrary, it would be perfectly consistent with his goal of creating a world in which his own interest are maximized. To be sure, he would have to be deceitful; in order to secure the good will of others, and a favorable hearing for his exhortations to altruism, he would have to pretend that he was himself prepared to accept altruistic principles. But again, that would be all right; from the egoist's point of view, this would merely be a matter of adopting the necessary means to the achievement of his goal—and while we might not approve of this, there is nothing inconsistent about it. Again, it might be said, "He advocates one thing, but does another. Surely *that's* inconsistent." But it is not; for what he advocates and what he does are both calculated as means to an end (the *same* end, we might note); and as such, he is doing what is rationally required in each case. Therefore, contrary to the previous argument, there is nothing inconsistent in the ethical egoist's view. He cannot be refuted by the claim that he contradicts himself.

Is there, then, no way to refute the ethical egoist? If by "refute" we mean show that he has made some *logical* error, the answer is that there is not. However, there is something more that can be said. The egoist challenge to our ordinary moral convictions amounts to a demand for an explanation of why we should adopt certain policies of action, namely policies in which the good of others is given importance. We can give an answer to this demand, albeit an indirect one. The reason one ought not to do actions that would hurt other people is: Other people would be hurt. The reason one ought to do actions that would benefit other people is: Other people would be benefited. This may at first seem like a piece of philosophical sleight-of-hand, but it is not. The point is that the welfare of human beings is something that most of us value *for its own sake*, and not merely for the sake of something else. Therefore, when *further* reasons are demanded for valuing the welfare of human beings, we cannot point to anything further to satisfy this demand. It is not that we have no reason for pursuing these policies, but that our reason *is* that these policies are for the good of human beings.

So if we are asked, "Why shouldn't I set fire to this department store?" one answer would be, "Because if you do, people may be burned to death." This is a complete, sufficient reason which does not require qualification or supplementation of any sort. If someone seriously wants to know why this action shouldn't be done, that's the reason. If we are pressed further and asked the skeptical question, "But why shouldn't I do actions that will harm others?" we may not know what to say—but this is because the questioner has included in his question the very answer we would like to give: "Why shouldn't you do actions that will harm others? Because doing those actions would harm others."

The egoist, no doubt, will not be happy with this. He will protest that *we* may accept this as a reason, but *he* does not. And here the argument stops: There are limits to what can be accomplished by argument, and if the egoist really doesn't care about other people—if he honestly doesn't care whether they are helped or hurt by his actions—then we have reached those limits. If we want to persuade him to act decently toward his fellow humans, we will have to make our appeal to such other attitudes as he does possess, by threats, bribes, or other cajolery. That is all that we can do.

Though some may find this situation distressing (we would like to be able to show that the egoist is just *wrong*), it holds no embarrassment for common morality. What we have come up against is simply a fundamental requirement of rational action, namely, that the existence of reasons for action always depends on the prior existence of certain attitudes in the agent. For example, the fact that a certain course of action would make the agent a lot of money is a reason for doing it only if the agent wants to make money; the fact that practicing at chess makes one a better player is a reason for practicing only if one wants to be a better player; and so on. Similarly, the fact that a certain action would help the agent is a reason for doing the action only if the agent cares about his own welfare, and the fact that an action would help others is a reason for doing it only if the agent cares about others. In this respect ethical egoism and what we might call ethical altruism are in exactly the same fix: Both require that the agent *care* about himself, or about other people, before they can get started.

So a nonegoist will accept "It would harm another person" as a reason not to do an action simply because he cares about what happens to that other person. When the egoist says that he does *not* accept that as a reason, he is saying something quite extraordinary. He is saying that he has no affection for friends or family, that he never feels pity or compassion, that he is the sort of person who can look on scenes of human misery with complete indifference, so long as he is not the one suffering. Genuine egoists, people who really don't care at all about anyone than themselves, are rare. It is important to keep this in mind when thinking about ethical egoism; it is easy to forget just how fundamental to human psychological makeup the feeling of sympathy is. Indeed, a man without any sympathy at all would scarcely be recognizable as a man; and that is what makes ethical egoism such a disturbing doctrine in the first place.

IV

There are, of course, many different ways in which the skeptic might challenge the assumptions underlying our moral practice. In this essay I have discussed only two of them, the two put forward by Glaucon in the passage that I cited from Plato's *Republic*. It is important that the assumptions underlying our moral practice should not be confused with particular judgments made within that practice. To defend one is not to defend the other. We may assume—quite properly, if my analysis has been correct—that the virtue of beneficence does, and indeed should, occupy an important place in "the moral institution of life"; and yet we may make constant and miserable errors when it comes to judging when and in what ways this virtue is to be exercised. Even worse, we may often be able to make accurate moral judgments, and know what we ought to do, but not do it. For these ills, philosophy alone is not the cure.

Morality, Egoism and the Prisoner's Dilemma

PETER SINGER

Peter Singer (b. 1946) teaches philosophy at La Trobe University in Victoria, Australia. His books include *Animal Liberation, Practical Ethics*, and *The Expanding Circle*.

Singer disputes Hobbes's claim that human beings are by nature antisocial and mutually hostile. He points out that ethical systems are found in all human communities, no matter how impoverished, debased, or decimated those communities may be. In response to the common assumption that all human beings are motivated by self-interest alone, Singer refers to a puzzle known as the

MORALITY, EGOISM AND THE PRISONER'S DILEMMA   Excerpts from *The Expanding Circle* by Peter Singer. Copyright © 1981 by Peter Singer. Reprinted by permission of Farrar, Straus, and Giroux, Inc.

Prisoner's Dilemma. This puzzle suggests that it will often be in our best interest *not* to be motivated by self-interest. And genuine altruism may have great evolutionary advantages for our species.

Every human society has some code of behavior for its members. This is true of nomads and city-dwellers, of hunter-gatherers and of industrial civilizations, of Eskimos in Greenland and Bushmen in Africa, of a tribe of twenty Australian aborigines and of the billion people that make up China. Ethics is part of the natural human condition.

That ethics is natural to human beings has been denied. More than three hundred years ago Thomas Hobbes wrote in his *Leviathan*:

> During the time men live without a common Power to keep them all in awe they are in that condition called War; and such a war, as is of every man against every other man. . . . To this war of every man against every man, this also is consequent; that nothing can be Unjust. The notions of Right and Wrong, Justice and Injustice have there no place.

Hobbes's guess about human life in the state of nature was no better than Rousseau's idea that we are naturally solitary. It is not the force of the state that persuades us to act ethically. The state, or some other form of social power, may reinforce our tendency to observe an ethical code, but that tendency exists before the social power is established. The primary role Hobbes gave to the state was always suspect on philosophical grounds, for it invites the question why, having agreed to set up a power to enforce the law, human beings would trust each other long enough to make the agreement work. Now we also have biological grounds for rejecting Hobbes's theory.

Occasionally there are claims that a group of human beings totally lacking any ethical code has been discovered. The Ik, a northern Uganda tribe described by Colin Turnbull in *The Mountain People*, is the most recent example. The biologist Garrett Hardin has even claimed that the Ik are an incarnation of Hobbes's natural man, living in a state of war of every Ik against every other

Ik. The Ik certainly were, at the time of Turnbull's visit, a most unfortunate people. Originally nomadic hunters and gatherers, their hunting ground was turned into a national park. They were forced to become farmers in an arid mountain area in which they had difficulty supporting themselves; a prolonged drought and consequent famine was the final blow. As a result, according to Turnbull, Ik society collapsed. Parents turned their three-year-old children out to fend for themselves, the strong took food from the mouths of the weak, the sufferings of the old and sick were a source of laughter, and anyone who helped another was considered a fool. The Ik, Turnbull says, abandoned family, cooperation, social life, love, religion, and everything else except the pursuit of self-interest. They teach us that our much vaunted human values are, in Turnbull's words, "luxuries that can be dispensed with."

The idea of a people without human values holds a certain repugnant fascination. *The Mountain People* achieved a rare degree of fame for a work of anthropology. It was reviewed in *Life*, talked about over cocktails, and turned into a stage play by the noted director Peter Brook. It was also severely criticized by some anthropologists. They pointed out the subjective nature of many of Turnbull's observations, the vagueness of his data, contradictions between *The Mountain People* and an earlier report Turnbull had published (in which he described the Ik as fun-loving, helpful, and "great family people"), and contradictions within *The Mountain People* itself. In reply Turnbull admitted that "the data in the book are inadequate for anything approaching proof" and recognized the existence of evidence pointing toward a different picture of Ik life.

Even if we take the picture of Ik life in *The Mountain People* at face value, there is still ample evidence that Ik society has an ethical code. Turbull refers to disputes over the theft of berries which reveal that, although stealing takes place, the Ik retain notions of private property and the wrongness of theft. Turnbull mentions the Ik's attachment to the mountains and the reverence with which they speak of Mount Morungole, which seems to be a sacred place for them. He observes that the Ik like to sit together in groups and insist on living together in villages. He describes a code that has to be followed by an Ik husband who intends to beat his wife, a code that gives the wife a chance to leave first. He reports that the obligations of a pact of mutual assistance known as *nyot* are invariably carried out. He tells us that there is a strict prohibition on Ik killing each other or even drawing blood. The Ik may let each other starve, but they apparently do not think of other Ik as they think of any non-human animals they find—that is, as potential food. A normal well-fed reader will take the prohibition of cannibalism for granted, but under the circumstances in which the Ik were living human flesh would have been a great boost to the diets of stronger Ik; that they refrain from this source of food is an example of the continuing strength of their ethical code despite the crumbling of almost everything that had made their lives worth living.

Under extreme conditions like those of the Ik during famine, the individual's need to survive becomes so dominant that it may seem as if all other values have ceased to matter, when in fact they continue to exercise an influence. If any conditions can be worse than those the Ik endured, they were the conditions of the inmates of Soviet labor camps and, more horrible still, the Nazi death camps. Here too, it has been said that "the doomed devoured each other," that "all trace of human solidarity vanished," that all values were erased and every man fought for himself. Nor should it be surprising if this were so, for the camps deliberately and systematically dehumanized their inmates, stripping them naked, shaving their hair, assigning them numbers, forcing them to soil their clothing with excrement, letting them know in a hundred ways that their lives were of no account, beating them, torturing them, and starving them. The astonishing thing is that despite all this, life in the camps was *not* every man for himself. Again and again, survivors' reports show that prisoners helped each other. In Auschwitz prisoners risked their lives to pick up strangers who had fallen in the snow at roll call; they built a radio and disseminated news to keep up morale; though they were starving, they shared food with those still more needy. There were also ethical rules in the camps. Though theft occurred, stealing from one's fellow prisoners was strongly condemned and those caught stealing were punished by the prisoners themselves. As Terrence Des Pres observes in *The Survivor*, a book based on reports by those who survived the camps: "The assumption that there was no moral or social order in the camps is wrong. . . . Through innumerable small acts of humanness, most of them covert but everywhere in evidence, survivors were able to maintain societal structures workable enough to keep themselves alive and morally sane."

The core of ethics runs deep in our species and is common to

human beings everywhere. It survives the most appalling hard-
ships and the most ruthless attempts to deprive human beings of
their humanity. . . .

The Prisoner's Dilemma

. . . [I]t is a common assumption that sociobiology implies that we
are motivated by self-interest, not by genuine altruism. This
assumption gains credibility from some of the things sociobiolo-
gists write. We can now see that sociobiology itself can explain the
existence of genuinely altruistic motivation. The implications of
this I shall take up in a later chapter, but it may be useful to make
the underlying mechanism more explicit. This can be done by
reference to a puzzle known as the Prisoner's Dilemma.

In the cells of the Ruritanian secret police are two political
prisoners. The police are trying to persuade them to confess to
membership in an illegal opposition party. The prisoners know that
if neither of them confesses, the police will not be able to make the
charge stick, but they will be interrogated in the cells for another
three months before the police give up and let them go. If one of
them confesses, implicating the other, the one who confesses will be
released immediately but the other will be sentenced to eight years
in jail. If both of them confess, their helpfulness will be taken into
account and they will get five years in jail. Since the prisoners are
interrogated separately, neither can know if the other has confessed
or not.

The dilemma is, of course, whether to confess. The point of the
story is that circumstances have been so arranged that if either
prisoner reasons from the point of view of self-interest, she will
find it to her advantage to confess; whereas taking the interests of
the two prisoners together, it is obviously in their interests if
neither confesses. Thus the first prisoner's self-interested calculations go like this: "If the other prisoner confesses, it will be better
for me if I have also confessed, for then I will get five years instead
of eight; and if the other prisoner does not confess, it will still be
better for me if I confess, for then I will be released immediately,
instead of being interrogated for another three months. Since we
are interrogated separately, whether the other prisoner confesses
has nothing to do with whether I confess—our choices are entirely

independent of each other. So whatever happens, it will be better for me if I confess." The second prisoner's self-interested reasoning will, of course, follow exactly the same route as the first prisoner's, and will come to the same conclusion. As a result, both prisoners, if self-interested, will confess, and both will spend the next five years in prison. There was a way for them both to be out in three months, but because they were locked into purely self-interested calculations, they could not take that route.

What would have to be changed in our assumptions about the prisoners to make it rational for them both to refuse to confess? One way of achieving this would be for the prisoners to make an agreement that would bind them both to silence. But how could each prisoner be confident that the other would keep the agreement? If one prisoner breaks the agreement, the other will be in prison for a long time, unable to punish the cheater in any way. So each prisoner will reason: "If the other one breaks the agreement, it will be better for me if I break it too; and if the other one keeps the agreement, I will still be better off if I break it. So I will break the agreement."

Without sanctions to back it up, an agreement is unable to bring two self-interested individuals to the outcome that is best for both of them, taking their interests together. What has to be changed to reach this result is the assumption that the prisoners are motivated by self-interest alone. If, for instance, they are altruistic to the extent of caring as much for the interests of their fellow prisoner as they care for their own interests, they will reason thus: "If the other prisoner does not confess it will be better for us both if I do not confess, for then between us we will be in prison for a total of six months, whereas if I do confess the total will be for eight years; and if the other prisoner does confess it will still be better if I do not confess, for then the total served will be eight years, instead of ten. So whatever happens, taking our interests together, it will be better if I don't confess." A pair of altruistic prisoners will therefore come out of this situation better than a pair of self-interested prisoners, *even from the point of view of self-interest.*

Altruistic motivation is not the only way to achieve a happier solution. Another possibility is that the prisoners are conscientious, regarding it as morally wrong to inform on a fellow prisoner; or if they are able to make an agreement, they might believe they have a duty to keep their promises. In either case, each will be able to rely on the other not confessing and they will be free in three months.

The Prisoner's Dilemma shows that, paradoxical as it may seem, we will sometimes be better off if we are not self-interested. Two or more people motivated by self-interest alone may not be able to promote their interests as well as they could if they were more altruistic or more conscientious.

The Prisoner's Dilemma explains why there could be an evolutionary advantage in being genuinely altruistic instead of making reciprocal exchanges on the basis of calculated self-interest. Prisons and confessions may not have played a substantial role in early human evolution, but other forms of cooperation surely did. Suppose two early humans are attacked by a sabertooth cat. If both flee, one will be picked off by the cat; if both stand their ground, there is a very good chance that they can fight the cat off; if one flees and the other stands and fights, the fugitive will escape and the fighter will be killed. Here the odds are sufficiently like those in the Prisoner's Dilemma to produce a similar result. From a self-interested point of view, if your partner flees your chances of survival are better if you flee too (you have a 50 percent chance rather than none at all) and if your partner stands and fights you still do better to run (you are sure of escape if you flee, whereas it is only probable, not certain, that together you and your partner can overcome the cat). So two purely self-interested early humans would flee, and one of them would die. Two early humans who cared for each other, however, would stand and fight, and most likely neither would die. Let us say, just to be able to put a figure on it, that two humans cooperating can defeat a sabertooth cat on nine out of every ten occasions and on the tenth occasion the cat kills one of them. Let us also say that when a sabertooth cat pursues two fleeing humans it always catches one of them, and which one it catches is entirely random, since differences in human running speed are negligible in comparison to the speed of the cat. Then one of a pair of purely self-interested humans would not, on average, last more than a single encounter with a sabertooth cat; but one of a pair of altruistic humans would on average survive ten such encounters.

If situations analogous to this imaginary sabertooth cat attack were common, early humans would do better hunting with altruistic comrades than with self-interested partners. Of course, an egoist who could find an altruist to go hunting with him would do better still; but altruists who could not detect—and refuse to assist—purely self-interested partners would be selected against. Evolution would therefore favor those who are genuinely altruistic to other genuine altruistics, but are not altruistic to those who seek to take advantage of their altruism. We can add, again, that the same goal could be achieved if, instead of being altruistic, early humans were moved by something like a sense that it is wrong to desert a partner in the face of danger.

Suggested Readings

Baier, Kurt. *The Moral Point of View.* Ithaca, N.Y.: Cornell University Press, 1958.

Bayles, Michael D., ed. *Contemporary Utilitarianism.* New York: Doubleday, 1968.

Benedict, Ruth. *Patterns of Culture.* Boston: Houghton Mifflin Co., 1934.

Blum, Lawrence. *Friendship, Altruism and Morality.* London: Routledge and Kegan Paul, 1980.

Caplan, Arthur L., ed. *The Sociobiology Debate: Readings on Ethical and Scientific Issues.* New York: Harper & Row, 1978.

Donagan, Alan. *The Theory of Morality.* Chicago: University of Chicago Press, 1977.

Frankena, William. *Ethics.* Englewood Cliffs, N.J.: Prentice-Hall, 1973.

Gert, Bernard. *The Moral Rules: A New Rational Foundation for Morality.* New York: Harper & Row, 1970.

Harman, Gilbert. *The Nature of Morality: An Introduction to Ethics.* New York: Oxford University Press, 1977.

Hospers, John. *Human Conduct.* New York: Harcourt Brace Jovanovich, 1961.

Ladd, John, ed. *Ethical Relativism.* Belmont, Calif.: Wadsworth Books, 1973.

MacIntyre, Alasdair. *A Short History of Ethics.* New York: Macmillan, 1966.

Mackie, J. L. *Ethics: Inventing Right and Wrong.* New York: Penguin Books, 1977.

Midgley, Mary. *Heart and Mind.* New York: St. Martin's Press, 1981.

————. *Wickedness.* London: Routledge and Kegan Paul, 1984.

Nagel, Thomas. *The Possibility of Altruism.* Oxford: Oxford University Press, 1970.

Singer, Marcus. *Generalization in Ethics.* New York: Alfred A. Knopf, 1961.

Singer, Peter. *The Expanding Circle: Ethics and Sociobiology.* New York: Farrar, Straus and Giroux, 1981.

Slote, Michael. *Goods and Virtues.* Oxford: Clarendon Press, 1983.

Smart, J. J. C., and Bernard Williams. *Utilitarianism: For and Against.* Cambridge: Cambridge University Press, 1973.

Warnock, G. J. *The Object of Morality.* London: Methuen and Co., 1971.

Williams, Bernard. *Ethics and the Limits of Philosophy.* Cambridge: Harvard University Press, 1985.

E 0
F 1
G 2
H 3
I 4
J